SEVENTH EDITION

WORKBOOK

PRACTICAL AVIATION & AEROSPACE LAW

J. Scott Hamilton

Sarah Nilsson

D1637467

AVIATION SUPPLIES & ACADEMICS
NEWCASTLE, WASHINGTON

J. Scott Hamilton is an adjunct professor and course developer at Embry-Riddle Aeronautical University, formerly assistant professor and faculty chair. He previously served as general counsel for the Civil Air Patrol, then as the national organization's chief operating officer. Prior to that, he served as senior assistant attorney general for the State of Wyoming. While practicing aviation law in Colorado, he also was a faculty member at the University of Denver College of Law, as well as Metropolitan State College of Denver. He is an experienced pilot and skydiver who served as a HALO instructor in the Green Berets. Hamilton is widely published on aviation law and has received many honors, including induction into the Colorado and Arkansas Aviation Halls of Fame.

Sarah Nilsson is an Assistant Professor at Embry-Riddle Aeronautical University and a practicing attorney in Arizona, where her practice focuses on aviation/aerospace and business law. She previously managed an Aerospace magnet program at an inner-city high school in Phoenix. Nilsson gained extensive aviation operating experience working as a cargo pilot and flight instructor and now volunteers as a safety representative on the FAA Safety Team. Her research interests include aviation, space, and unmanned aircraft systems law.

In 2017, Sarah published *Drones Across America* with the American Bar Association, a textbook devoted to Federal, State and local unmanned aircraft regulations, laws, and ordinances. Since 2015, she has been interviewed by news media on TV and radio and has presented at numerous conferences and symposia across the nation for The Citadel, the Arizona Attorney General's Office, Arizona Geographic Information Council, and the Air and Space Law Forum of the American Bar Association, to name a few.

Practical Aviation & Aerospace Law Workbook, Seventh Edition
J. Scott Hamilton, Sarah Nilsson

© 2020 Aviation Supplies & Academics, Inc.
All rights reserved.
Seventh Edition published 2020 by ASA.

Aviation Supplies & Academics, Inc.
7005 132nd Place SE
Newcastle, WA 98059
Email: asa@asa2fly.com
Website: www.asa2fly.com

Cover: bigstockphoto.com ©denbelitsky

ASA-PRCT-AV-WK7
ISBN 978-1-64425-032-7

Additional formats available:
Kindle   ISBN 978-1-64425-034-1
eBook ePub ISBN 978-1-64425-033-4
eBook PDF   ISBN 978-1-64425-035-8
eBundle   ISBN 978-1-64425-036-5 (print + eBook PDF download code)

Printed in the United States of America

2024   2023   2022   2021   9 8 7 6 5 4 3 2

CONTENTS

PREFACE

This WORKBOOK is designed to be used with the textbook *Practical Aviation & Aerospace Law, Seventh Edition*, in aviation and aerospace law courses offered to students preparing for careers in the aviation and aerospace industries. It helps you practice applying the legal principles discussed in the text to the kinds of decisions you will be making in the "real world" of aviation and aerospace as business and airport managers, pilots, maintenance personnel, air traffic controllers, security personnel, and the like.

Many of the workbook questions are based on real dilemmas our clients have faced over the years, while others are the product of a fertile imagination. In the classroom or online, your professor may introduce hypothetical changes to the facts given here, challenging you to analyze the effects that changes in facts (sometimes subtle) have on strategies and outcomes, and may bring particular, actual cases into the discussion.

This edition of the workbook also adds some suggested online research assignments that your professor may assign, usually to either explore changes that may occur after the textbook is published, or to take a more global view of the particular topic.

Because the workbook is closely keyed to the text, we suggest that as soon as you have read a chapter in the text, you work through the workbook questions on that chapter while it is fresh in your mind.

PART I

Administrative Law

1

REGULATORY AGENCIES AND INTERNATIONAL ORGANIZATIONS

Review Questions

1. You are the human resources director for a regional U.S. airline. One of your duties includes screening new pilots and maintenance personnel applying for jobs with the airline. As part of the process, your staff should check the FAA's records on each applicant's certificates, ratings, accident history, and FAR violation history. Where would they find this information?

2. You are an engineer for an avionics company that is designing a new navigational system for civil aviation use. What organization establishes the technical specifications for radio aids to navigation? In what series of publications would you look to find these specifications?

3. Your aircraft has been involved in an accident. What agency or agencies will investigate the accident? What agency will determine the *probable cause* of the accident?

4. An agency of the U.S. government is presently experimenting with and assisting in the development of technical standards for the components of the next generation air traffic control system (NextGen). What agency is responsible for that work, and where is it being carried out?

5. An agency of the U.S. government is conducting research and experimentation on methods for detecting airframe ice and conveying the information to the flight crew in a useful format. What agency would be responsible for such experimentation? If that research and experimentation leads to a new technology, what agency of the U.S. government would establish the airworthiness standards for incorporating that technology into U.S. civil aircraft?

6. An emerging nation wishes to enter into an agreement with the United States to facilitate regular airline service between the two nations. Which of the so-called "five freedoms of the air" would this involve? What agency of the U.S government would it deal with to negotiate a treaty to provide such service? Once the treaty has been negotiated, is any further action by the U.S. government required to bring it into effect?

7. The treaty (discussed above) providing for reciprocal air service is now in effect. The other nation wishes to designate its new national airline to provide a portion of the service under that agreement. Does the U.S. government have any say whether that airline will be permitted to provide that service to the United States? If so, how?

8. What has proved to be the most intractable problem facing international civil aviation on which to gain global agreement? Why?

9. Does the National Transportation Safety Board (NTSB) have any aviation responsibilities not relating directly to aircraft accidents? If so, describe.

10. Does the National Aeronautics and Space Administration (NASA) have any aviation responsibilities other than technological and aerodynamic research and development? If so, describe.

11. What are the powers of the Civil Aeronautics Board (CAB) today?

12. To what extent, if any, may state governments regulate the routes served and rates charged by airlines?

13. Which agency of the U.S. government regulates labor relations in the airline industry?

14. What authority, if any, does the National Labor Relations Board (NLRB) have over labor relations in:

    a. The airline industry?

    b. Aerospace manufacturing?

    c. General aviation?

15. Which agency of the U.S government has the primary responsibility for regulating aviation safety?

16. Describe and distinguish FAA and NASA responsibilities in regulating commercial spaceflight operations.

17. Distinguish U.S. Customs and Border Protection (CBP) responsibilities from those of Immigration and Customs Enforcement (ICE).

18. You want to determine who owns a particular aircraft. Which agency of the U.S. government would have that information, and where would it be found?

19. Until Congress passed and the president signed the Airline Deregulation Act of 1978, which agency of the U.S. government regulated airline economics (routes served and rates charged)?

20. Which agency or agencies of the U.S. government operate radio aids to air navigation?

21. Are there any privately owned and operated radio aids to navigation in the United States?

22. If the FAA and its counterpart agencies in other nations were interested in collaborating to make civil aircraft certification standards globally uniform, what organization would logically coordinate that effort? Where is that organization headquartered?

23. Why did the nations represented at the 1944 Chicago Conference not agree to the "five freedoms of the air" then proposed by the United States? If a similar conference were held today, do you think the international community would take the same position? Why?

24. Which agency of the U.S. government and which office of that agency is responsible for the production of aeronautical charts?

25. NASA research relating to general aviation focuses on what areas?

26. Which agency of the U.S. government is responsible for the day-to-day screening of airline passengers, baggage, and cargo?

27. That agency is now included in what federal department?

28. Is the regulation of workplace safety and health conditions in the U.S. preempted (regulated exclusively by) the federal government, or do the states have a role?

29. What federal agency is responsible for assuring the coordination and sharing of intelligence relating to threats against transportation?

30. What federal agency and what office of that agency is responsible for screening foreign applicants to U.S. flight schools for security risks?

31. Airlines providing international air service to the U.S. are required to transmit crew and passenger manifests electronically to what federal agency, prior to departure?

32. What are "open skies" agreements?

Online Research Assignments

As assigned by your instructor, prepare to present in class or post online one or more of the following research assignments, including hyperlinks to all online resources relied on:

1. For any one of the U.S. federal agencies identified in this chapter, identify the head of the agency by name and title, describe that person's background and qualifications, and include an image of that person.

2. For a nation or union of nations other than the U.S., identify a government agency that performs functions equivalent to those provided in the U.S. by the FAA; then identify the head of that agency by name and title, describe that person's background and qualifications, and include an image of that person.

3. Describe the goals, methods, status, and projected implementation of the FAA's NextGen ATC system, discussing the expected benefits and costs to system users.

4. Update the progress of International Civil Aviation Organization (ICAO) efforts to achieve global agreement on regulating greenhouse gas (GHG) emissions by civil aircraft and the status of application of the European Union's Emissions Trading Scheme (ETS) to civil aircraft.

5. Describe in detail the current status of FAA efforts to safely integrate operations of civil unmanned aircraft into the U.S. National Airspace System.

6. Describe activities and efforts of ICAO to achieve global uniformity on standards for and regulation of civil unmanned aircraft operations.

2

FAA ENFORCEMENT

Review Questions

1. You are flying a private aircraft from Salt Lake City, Utah to Los Angeles, California, under Visual Flight Rules (VFR). Over the Mojave Desert, you contact Los Angeles Center and request radar flight following to the Camarillo Airport. Center assigns you a transponder code with instructions to "squawk ident" and a moment later the pleasant sounding controller advises you: "Radar contact 3 miles north of the Mojave Airport. We had a report that you may have entered restricted airspace, so please give us a call at 213-666-1234 when you get on the ground."

   a. What will you reply? Why?

   b. What do you intend to do once you arrive at your destination? Why?

   c. After landing, you are tying down the aircraft when a person approaches and asks: "FAA. Are you the pilot of this aircraft?" What will you reply? What will you do? Why?

   d. The FAA inspector then asks: "May I see your airman and medical certificates and the aircraft registration and airworthiness certificates, please?" What will you say? What will you do? Why?

e. The inspector, who is now holding your documents, states: "I'm going to need to take these back to the office to make some copies. If you'll give me the address where you're staying, I'll have them returned to you in a couple of hours." What will you say? What will you do? Why?

f. The inspector ignores your response and heads for the parking lot with your documents. What will you do? Why?

g. Now the inspector turns nice, almost apologetic, saying: "Look, I think you're blowing this way out of proportion. We received an incident report and I have to investigate it. The sooner I get your answers to a few questions, the sooner I can complete my report and close the file on this. Now, where did you just fly this airplane in from?" Is the inspector lying to you about closing the file? What will you reply? Why?

h. The inspector departs. Are there any other actions that you have not yet taken but should? If so, describe each and state the reason for it.

i. A few days later, you receive a phone call from a person who identifies himself as an FAA inspector and inquires: "I've been assigned to investigate a report that you flew through Restricted Area R-2505 over by Nellis Air Force Base without permission. What can you tell me about that?" What will you reply? Why?

j. Three weeks later, you receive a letter from the FAA inspector (Figure WB 2-1). Are you required to respond to this letter? If you do, can your response be used as evidence to suspend or revoke your pilot certificate? What will you do now? Why?

U.S. Department
of Transportation

Federal Aviation
Administration

Western-Pacific Region

P.O. Box 92007
Worldway Postal Center
Los Angeles, CA 90009

July 5, 2019

File Number: 91WP123456

Your Name
Your Address
Anywhere, U.S.A. 98765

Dear (You):

Personnel of this office are investigating an incident
occurring on July 4, 2019, which involved the operation of
Cessna aircraft N57785 in the vicinity of Death Valley,
California, at approximately 3:15 p.m.

The aircraft was observed and identified as having entered
Restricted Area R-2505 without permission of the controlling
agency. Operation of this type is contrary to the Federal
Aviation Regulations.

This letter is to inform you that this matter is under
investigation by the Federal Aviation Administration. We
would appreciate receiving any evidence or statements you
might care to make regarding this matter within 10 days of
receipt of this letter. Any discussion or written statements furnished by you will be given consideration in our
investigation. If we do not hear from you within the specified time, our report will be processed without the benefit
of your statement.

Sincerely,

Maxwell R. Hardnasty
Aviation Safety Inspector

Figure WB 2-1. FAA letter of investigation.

2. You are flying a corporate turboprop from Miami to Chicago under Instrument Flight Rules (IFR). Your course takes you through a cold front with imbedded thunderstorms. ATC clears you to climb and maintain Flight Level (FL) 190. You encounter moderate to occasionally severe turbulence in strong updrafts and downdrafts along the front. You have slowed the aircraft to its turbulence penetration speed to avoid overstressing the airframe when you encounter the strongest updraft yet just as you are approaching your assigned altitude. You are using all of your skill and knowledge trying to arrest your ascent without exceeding the aircraft's turbulence penetration speed, but the updraft carries you above your assigned altitude. Just then, the controller calls and instructs you to "say altitude." Glancing at the encoding altimeter, you see that you are at FL 200 and have just begun a gradual descent with the power levers retarded to flight idle. You cannot descend more rapidly without exceeding turbulence penetration speed and thereby risking structural failure if more turbulence is encountered.

   a. What will you respond to ATC? Why?

   b. If you were expecting to encounter turbulence or updrafts and downdrafts that might make altitude holding difficult while traversing this area of bad weather, what could you have done before reaching the area to give yourself more vertical maneuvering room?

   c. As a result of the altitude deviation, what actions will you take after landing? Why?

3. You are the pilot in command of a light twin arriving VFR on a cross-country flight with radar flight following in an unfamiliar area. Visual Meteorological Conditions (VMC) prevail, though visibility is marginal at 3 to 5 miles. ATC advises you that your destination airport, an uncontrolled field, is "12 o'clock and 10 miles." Moments later, you see an airport straight ahead with the expected runway orientation, report the airport in sight, and land. Then you realize you've landed at the wrong airport and that your destination is several miles beyond this one.

   a. What will you do and why?

b. A few weeks later, you receive a letter from the FAA (Figure WB 2-2). Are you required to comply? If you comply, who must pay for the aircraft for the reexamination?

c. If you do not promptly submit to the requested reexamination, what can the FAA do about it?

4. You are an aircraft mechanic with airframe and powerplant (A&P) ratings. You work the night shift at a shop that does a high volume of inspections and maintenance on a wide variety of general aviation aircraft. You are awakened at home at 8:00 a.m. by a phone call from a person who identifies herself as an FAA inspector and asks: "Did you perform a left wing repair on Cessna N7173M?"

a. What will you reply? Why?

b. What else will you do? Why?

5. You have inadvertently violated an FAR.

a. If the FAA doesn't know about your violation, will it find out because you file an Aviation Safety Report with NASA?

b. Should you wait until you find out whether the FAA is going to take some enforcement action against you before filing a NASA Aviation Safety Report? Why?

c. If the FAA finds out about the violation, what difference will it make if you have filed an Aviation Safety Report with NASA?

U.S Department
of Transportation

Federal Aviation
Administration

Flight Standards District Office
116 North 2400 West
Salt Lake City, Utah 84116

January 15, 2019

File Number: 91GL123457

Your Name
Your Address
Anywhere, U.S.A. 98765

Dear (You):

Investigation of an incident that occurred at Wrong Field
Municipal Airport at Dayton, Ohio, on December 25, 2018,
gives reason to believe that your competence as a certificated airman is in question and that reexamination of your
qualification to be the holder of a private pilot certificate is necessary in the interest of safety.

Therefore, pursuant to the authority contained in Section
609 of the Federal Aviation Act of 1958, as amended, you are
requested to call or appear at this office or a Flight
Standards District Office more conveniently located to you
no later than January, 25, 2019, to make an appointment for
a reexamination. The reexamination will consist of an oral
examination and flight test to include the knowledge and
skill necessary to be the holder of a private pilot certificate, with emphasis on pre-flight planning, navigation, and
airport identification. If you make an appointment with a
Flight Standards District Office in another area, please
advise this office.

Your cooperation in this matter will be appreciated.

Sincerely,

Maxwell R. Hardnasty
Aviation Safety Inspector

Figure WB 2-2. FAA reexamination letter.

d. What are the disadvantages of filing an Aviation Safety Report with NASA?

e. May you be able to qualify for remedial training instead of suspension or revocation of your pilot certificate? Why?

6. You receive a Notice of Proposed Certificate Action signed by an FAA attorney notifying you that the FAA believes you have violated one or more FARs and intends to suspend your certificate for 180 days. A form is attached that offers you the opportunity for an informal conference with the FAA attorney.

   a. What is the purpose of an informal conference?

   b. Can statements you make at the informal conference later be used by the FAA as evidence against you?

   c. If the informal conference does not lead to the resolution of the case, what will be the FAA's next move?

7. The FAA issues an Order of Suspension against your certificate.

   a. Do you have the right to appeal that order? If so, to whom?

   b. Who will hear the "trial" of your appeal and make the initial decision?

   c. Do you have the right to a jury trial at any point in an appeal from an FAA certificate action?

d. Who has the burden of proof at the hearing? Must your guilt be proved beyond a reasonable doubt?

e. If, after hearing the evidence, the judge feels that the FAA is being too soft on you, does the judge have the authority to impose a longer period of suspension than the FAA has ordered or to order revocation of your certificate instead of suspension?

f. Does the judge have the authority to change the suspension to a fine?

g. Can the judge's initial decision be appealed further? If so, by whom and to whom?

h. Will you get a new hearing at that next level of appeal?

i. Can the full NTSB's decision be appealed further? If so, by whom and to whom?

j. Will you get a new trial on that appeal?

k. Can the decision on that appeal be appealed any further? If so, by whom and to whom?

l. When do you have to stop exercising the privileges of your certificate and serve the period of suspension imposed?

8. If the FAA issues an Order of Suspension with Waiver of Sanction, waiving the sanction because you timely filed an Aviation Safety Report with NASA, can you still appeal the order through the process described above in an effort to keep the regulatory violation(s) charged off your record? If so, what is the worst that could happen to you as a result of that appeal?

9. Can the FAA both suspend your certificate and fine you as punishment for the same FAR violation? Why?

10. Can the FAA both require you to submit to reexamination and suspend your certificate for the same FAR violation? Why?

11. If the FAA issues an Emergency Order of Suspension or Revocation against your certificate, how will the procedure differ from that described in your answer to Question 7?

12. You have passed the written exam for the Airline Transport Pilot (ATP) certificate and need only an additional 20 hours of flight time to qualify to take the oral and flight tests. You are offered a dream job, but the catch is that you must have your ATP in hand by the first of the month or they will hire someone else for the position. You are out of work and broke and couldn't afford to fly even if the weather cooperated (which it doesn't look like it's going to), so you feel a strong temptation to "pad" your logbooks with 20 hours of imaginary flying and present them to the FAA with your application to take the ATP oral and flight tests. If you do this and your padding is discovered, what are the probable consequences to you?

13. You are a certificated pilot, but do not hold an instrument rating. On a pretty summer day, you intentionally fly through a puffy little white cumulus cloud, just to see what it's like. If you file an Aviation Safety Report with NASA upon landing, will that protect you from any possible punishment for your violation of the cloud clearance requirements published in the basic VFR weather minimums of 14 CFR §91.155? Why?

14. You are the director of maintenance for a regional airline. You are informed by one of the company's mechanics that she has just discovered that one of the company's aircraft has overflown the time it was due for performance of an FAA Airworthiness Directive (AD) by almost 100 hours. What will you do? Why?

15. The NTSB doctrine of "*due deference*" allowed the FAA to do what? What effect did the Pilot's Bill of Rights have on this?

16. What did Congress intend to accomplish by enacting the "Hoover Bill"? Do you think it worked?

17. The FAA suspended your certificate for 180 days for an FAR violation. Because you either failed to timely appeal the Order of Suspension or you have exhausted the appeal process and the FAA prevailed, the order is final. How long will the violation remain on your FAA record?

Online Research Assignments

As assigned by your instructor, prepare to present in class or post online one or more of the following research assignments, including hyperlinks to all online resources relied on:

1. Select a U.S. state that has some significance to you. Assume that you have received an FAA Order of Suspension for an alleged FAR violation, appealed that decision to the NTSB, and an NTSB Administrative Law Judge (ALJ) will hold a hearing on your case in that state. Using the NTSB website **http://www.ntsb.gov/legal/alj/Pages/judges.aspx** determine which ALJ is assigned to the Circuit that includes your state and that judge's background and qualifications.

2. Select a nation or union of nations other than the U.S. and determine for that nation:

   a. The government entity that issues and enforces national civil aviation safety regulations.

   b. The process of investigation, accusation, and appeal of reports of that nation's civil aviation safety regulations.

3. Identify and brief a recent full NTSB or U.S. Court of Appeals decision of an FAR violation case involving operation of a civil unmanned aircraft, including:

   a. The name of the case

   b. The entity (full NTSB or Court) deciding the case

   c. FAR violations charged

   d. Legal issues

   e. Decision-maker's analysis of the issues

   f. Decision

3

AVIATION MEDICAL CASES

Review Questions

1. You have failed the color-vision test during your examination for an aviation medical certificate. Is there another procedure by which you may still be able to obtain an aviation medical certificate? If so, explain.

2. You are suffering from what you think is a bad cold and are taking a cold remedy.

    a. How can you tell if it is legal for you to fly while you are taking that medication?

    b. Even if it is technically legal for you to fly, is it prudent? Why?

3. You hold an unexpired aviation medical certificate when you experience a health problem.

    a. Describe the complete analytical process by which you will determine whether or not it is legal for you to continue to act as a pilot or other required flight crewmember.

    b. Are you required to report a change in your health to the FAA?

c. Are there any events that might occur in your life that you are required to report to the FAA prior to your next aviation medical exam? If so, describe.

d. If your condition would disqualify you from acting as a pilot or required flight crewmember, are you required to surrender your aviation medical certificate to the FAA?

e. If your condition would disqualify you from acting as a pilot or required flight crewmember but you go ahead and do so anyway, what are the possible legal consequences to you?

4. You are arrested for an alcohol or drug-related traffic offense.

a. Are you required to report the arrest to the FAA? If so, to whom and when?

b. If the arrest leads to your conviction of a drug- or alcohol-related traffic offense, are you required to report the conviction to the FAA? If so, to whom and when?

c. If the arrest leads to the suspension or revocation of your driver's license, are you required to report that administrative action to the FAA? If so, to whom and when?

d. Because this is your first offense, your attorney is able to negotiate a settlement agreement whereby your case will be dismissed with no conviction, so long as you attend an approved driver's education or drug or alcohol rehab program and have no further drug- or alcohol-related arrests within the next year. Are you required to report that result to the FAA? If so, to whom and when?

e. You receive a letter from the FAA requesting that you submit to a rather extensive and expensive battery of psychological and psychiatric tests to determine whether you are an alcoholic. Are you required to comply? If you comply, who is responsible to pay for these tests?

f. What are the possible legal consequences to you, if any, if you fail to promptly comply with the FAA's request?

5. Your aviation medical exam reveals evidence of coronary artery disease. Your Aviation Medical Examiner (AME) denies your application for an aviation medical certificate and refers you to a cardiologist. On the cardiologist's recommendation, you undergo heart surgery. The procedure goes well, and your postoperative course is also smooth. You have quit smoking, gone on a low-cholesterol diet, and have been following a good exercise regimen. Your cardiologist expresses the opinion that so long as you continue your new healthier lifestyle, you are no more likely to experience a heart attack than the average person of your age not having your medical history.

a. Do you now have a right to an aviation medical certificate?

b. Is there a procedure by which you may obtain aviation medical certification? If so, describe.

6. You are a pilot for a U.S. airline, flying international routes. On a layover in a third world country, you experience crushing chest pain and become violently ill. You are taken to a crude local medical clinic, where the doctor tells you that you suffered a heart attack. The next morning, you feel fine, so you are convinced the doctor's diagnosis was in error. The doctor, however, adamantly stands by his diagnosis.

a. Is it legal for you to act as a pilot or other required flight crewmember on the return flight to the U.S.? Why?

b. Are you required to report this event and diagnosis to the FAA? If so, to whom and when?

c. When you return to the U.S., you undergo a thorough cardiovascular evaluation. At the conclusion of the testing, the cardiologist explains to you that a heart attack results from something blocking one of the coronary arteries that supply oxygenated blood to the heart muscle, causing the portion of the muscle that is deprived of its blood supply to die. Physicians refer to this as a "myocardial infarction" and the tests you took would have revealed the presence of any such dead tissue. No such damage appeared on your tests, so your cardiologist states with confidence that the foreign doctor's diagnosis was in error; you did not experience a heart attack. If the FAA denies your application for aviation medical certification or revokes your current aviation medical certificate based on the foreign diagnosis, is there a procedure through which you may still be able to obtain or retain your aviation medical certificate? If so, describe.

7. On the Application for Aviation Medical Certificate (textbook Figure 3-2) you must report, among many other things, any arrest or conviction involving driving while intoxicated by, impaired by, or under the influence of alcohol or a drug and any resulting denial, suspension, cancellation, or revocation of driving privileges or attendance at an educational or rehabilitation program.

a. Why are these questions on the Application for Aviation Medical Certificate?

b. If you have such a record, but fail to report it on your application, is the FAA likely to find out about it? If so, how?

c. What are the possible legal consequences, if any, if you have such a record but fail to report it on your application?

8. You are a corporate pilot, working as captain of a 2-person flight deck crew on a business jet that requires 2 pilots. You hold an FAA ATP certificate and your first officer holds an FAA commercial pilot certificate. You both hold Class 2 FAA airman medical certificates and are both type-rated in the business jet. The corporation you both work for has been operating only within the U.S., but is about to expand its reach (and the routes you'll be flying) globally. Should either or both of you make any change to your FAA airman medical certification? Explain.

Online Research Assignments

As assigned by your instructor, prepare to present in class or post online one or more of the following research assignments, including hyperlinks to all online resources relied on:

1. Select a nation or union of nations other than the U.S. and compare that nation's medical standards for certification of civilian pilots with the FAA health standards discussed in this chapter.

2. Identify and describe a fatal civil aviation accident (anywhere on the globe) that was determined to have been caused by a flight crewmember's medical condition and discuss recommendations that were made (if any) to prevent a similar tragedy. Have those recommendations been implemented?

3. Determine whether there is a free online source for the full text of ICAO Annex 1 —"Medical Assessment Process and ATOs."

PART II

Aircraft Accidents

4

BASIC PRINCIPLES OF CIVIL LIABILITY

Review Questions

1. What is a *tort*?

2. What is *negligence*?

3. What are the four elements a plaintiff must prove in order to win a lawsuit for negligence?

4. Under what circumstances is a business legally liable for the consequences of the negligence of its employees?

5. You are the general manager of a fixed base operation (FBO). Your shop performed an annual inspection on a customer's airplane and released the airplane to the customer when the job was completed, but before your bill was paid. Later, the customer complained that the bill was excessive, and refused to pay it. Arriving for work one morning, you notice the airplane parked in one of the airport's transient parking spots, unattended. The thought occurs to you to tow the airplane into your hangar, lock it up, and refuse to release it until the bill is paid. Is this a prudent course of action? Explain.

6. You are a commercial balloon pilot in the business of flying couples on romantic champagne balloon flights. One morning, while aloft on such a flight over a picturesque valley of farms and vineyards, the wind suddenly shifts direction and begins to increase, carrying the balloon toward the nearby ocean. Rather than risk being swept out to sea, you quickly descend and land in a vineyard. The gondola leaves a swath of broken and uprooted grapevines before it drags to a halt and the balloon envelope deflates. You and your passengers emerge scratched, bruised, and shaken, but otherwise unhurt just as your ground crew pulls up in their four-wheel-drive truck, having torn their own swath through the vineyard while racing in to help you. Your crew has just begun gathering up the balloon when the enraged vintner arrives, jumping out of his Jeep brandishing a shotgun. Loudly pumping the shotgun's action to chamber a shell, the landowner levels the weapon on you and orders: "Just leave that damn thing where it lies, leave your truck where it sits, and start walking. I want all of you off my property right now before you do any more damage."

   a. Have you, the pilot, committed an intentional tort? Explain.

   b. Has your ground crew committed an intentional tort? Explain.

   c. Has the landowner committed an intentional tort? Explain.

   d. Were you, the pilot, negligent?

   e. Do you have any legal defense that might keep you from having to pay for the damage to the grapevines (which can be very expensive)? Explain.

   f. You are holding the magnum of champagne. Just as a member of your ground crew distracts the landowner, it occurs to you that you could just bop the old fool over the head with the champagne bottle, take away his shotgun, and be on your way without further hassle. What will you do? Why?

7. If you are involved in an aircraft accident causing injuries to other people or damage to their property and you are convicted of an FAR violation in connection with that accident, will that conviction have any effect on the outcome of a civil lawsuit against you for negligence? Explain.

8. What is the common theme running through all American law—administrative, civil, and criminal?

9. To whom do you owe a duty to be reasonably careful?

10. You are involved in an aircraft accident that causes injuries to other people or damage to their property. The NTSB finds that the probable cause of the accident was pilot error on your part. Will the NTSB's finding of probable cause be admissible as evidence in a civil trial against you for negligence to prove the proximate (legal) cause of the accident? Will other evidence from the NTSB's investigation and report be admissible in evidence in that civil trial? Explain.

11. Persons and businesses engaged in some types of activities face the risk of being held liable for injuries to others, even if the injuries are not proved to have resulted from some negligence on their part; this is called *strict liability*. What kinds of activities expose persons and businesses to the risk of being held strictly liable for injuries to others?

12. A general aviation manufacturer delivers a new eight-seat twin-engine FAA-certified aircraft to a buyer today. If there is a defect in the airplane when it is delivered, is the manufacturer potentially liable for injuries that may eventually be caused by that defect, no matter when the resulting harm occurs? Explain.

13. The Pentagon is in the market for a new light armed reconnaissance helicopter. Weight is a major consideration in the design because they want to be able to transport six of these helicopters at one time in a C-17 transport. Standard aeronautical engineering practice is to fabricate military aircraft fuel lines from steel, to improve occupant survivability in the event of a fire resulting from battle damage or accident. (Steel fuel lines are sufficiently heat resistant to allow the aircraft's occupants time to escape before the lines melt, feeding the fire and possibly causing an explosion.) Because of the weight considerations, the Pentagon has specified the use of aluminum fuel lines (which are much less heat resistant) in the new helicopter. If a manufacturer builds these helicopters in accordance with these military specifications and one crashes, incinerating its occupants because the aluminum fuel lines did not allow them time to escape from the aircraft, is the manufacturer potentially liable for a defective product? Are there any steps the manufacturer could take to avoid such liability? Explain.

14. In the process of repairing wing damage to an airplane, a repair station's employees inadvertently reversed the aileron cables to that wing and failed to catch their error upon completion of the work. When the owner picked up the airplane, he also failed to detect the discrepancy during his preflight inspection, with the result that moments after liftoff he found he had no control over the aircraft in the roll axis and crashed, destroying the aircraft and seriously injuring himself. He sues the repair station for negligence. The jury finds that the proximate cause of the accident was 60% the fault of the repair station and 40% the fault of the owner/pilot and that the pilot's damages (including loss of the aircraft) amount to $1,000,000. How much must the repair station pay the owner/pilot?

15. Approaching an airport to land, at about 1,000 feet above ground level (AGL), an airliner suddenly rolled inverted, entered a vertical dive, and dove straight into the ground. There were no survivors. The NTSB is unable to determine the probable cause of the crash. Is there any way for survivors of the passengers who were killed to prevail in litigation? If so, against whom? Explain.

16. You were the pilot of an aircraft that crashed, injuring passengers.

    a. You receive a Summons and Complaint in a civil suit brought by one of the passengers who alleges that your negligence caused the crash, seeking judgment against you for hundreds of thousands of dollars in damages for that passenger's injuries. What should you do? When? Why?

    b. At trial, how will the jury (none of whom will be pilots or have any aviation expertise) determine whether you were negligent?

    c. Will your attorney have the opportunity to find out what the other side intends to prove, and how, before trial? If so, describe.

    d. If you win the case, who will have to pay your attorney's fee? Who will have to pay them if you lose? Explain.

17. Running well ahead of schedule due to an extreme tailwind, a pilot employed by an air parcel service decides to make an unscheduled stop at an airport along his route to pay a surprise visit to an old college friend who works for an FBO there. Taxiing too fast for conditions on the icy ramp, the pilot loses control of the aircraft, colliding with a parked aircraft owned by the FBO. Is the pilot's employer liable to the FBO for the damage? Explain.

18. A business jet operated by a corporation from Nation A crashes on approach to landing in Nation B, demolishing a number of homes and businesses and killing and injuring numerous individuals on the ground. If both Nations A and B have signed the Rome Convention, are the persons and businesses harmed required to prove that some act of negligence by the aircraft operator caused the crash in order to receive compensation?

Online Research Assignments

As assigned by your instructor, prepare to present in class or post online the following research assignment, including hyperlinks to all online resources relied on:

1. In Review Question 18, your native country is Nation A. Select another nation where a business jet from your country might have reason to land. That becomes Nation B.

   a. Determine whether either or both of these nations is a signatory to the Rome Convention.

   b. If either or both Nations A and B are not signatories to the Rome Convention:

      i. How will the issue of legal liability for the damage and injuries to persons and property on the surface be resolved?

      ii. Analyze whether it is or would be advantageous or disadvantageous for the non-signatory nation(s) to sign the Rome Convention? Explain.

   c. If both Nations A and B are signatories to the Rome Convention, is this preferable to being non-signatories? Explain.

5

ORGANIZING THE BUSINESS TO LIMIT LIABILITY

Review Questions

1. What are the primary forms of business organization?

2. From a risk-management standpoint, which form or forms of business organization serve to protect the owners from personal vicarious liability for torts committed by employees acting within the scope of their employment and from business debts?

3. Can your chosen form of business protect you from personal liability for the consequences of your own negligence or intentional torts?

4. What are owners of a corporation called?

5. Regardless of its form, what duties does every business owe to its employees?

6. What is the *alter ego* doctrine?

7. What test does the Internal Revenue Service (IRS) apply to determine whether a person is an independent contractor or an employee of a business?

8. Does the IRS have the authority to determine that a person is (or was) an employee of the business rather than an independent contractor even if the business had an agreement signed by that worker stating that she is an independent contractor?

9. What difference does it make to a business whether the IRS considers a worker an employee of the business or an independent contractor?

10. Congratulations! You have been hired as a new assistant manager for an FBO. You learn that the business treats its aircraft salespersons, flight instructors, and aircraft mechanics as independent contractors. You ask your boss why and are told: "It saves us having to do all the paperwork and bear the extra expense of withholding payroll taxes and having to pay for workers' compensation insurance and unemployment compensation insurance premiums, and it keeps them from getting any ideas about joining a union." Do you think there's something wrong with that? Reply thoughtfully and in detail, as a model manager would.

11. In a corporation,
    a. What decisions do shareholders have the right to make?

b. What decisions do the board of directors typically make?

c. What decisions do corporate officers typically make?

12. You are the Vice President for Finance of JetLink, Inc., a regional airline. You are convinced that it would be prudent for the corporation to order 25 turboprop aircraft and sell an equal number of its regional jets, which are much more expensive to operate.

a. Who would you expect to have the authority to make the decision whether to implement your recommendation? Why?

b. Should there be some written record of that decision? If so, describe.

c. You are properly authorized to sign a purchase contract for those turboprops. How should your signature appear on that contract? Illustrate.

13. Why is it important to keep the corporation's money and other assets clearly separated from your own?

14. Refer to the letter from the president (CEO) of International Aviation Corporation (*see* Figure WB 5-1). Identify all legal errors in the letter, and correct each one by editing.

International Aviation

312 Earhart Way

Houston Intercontinental Airport

Houston, TX 77025

(713) 438-2255

January 15, 2015

Pratt & Whitney Aircraft Engines, Inc.
400 Main Street
East Hartford, CT 06108

Dear Sirs:
This is to confirm my order of eight (8) PW 4000 engines with accessories at the agreed price of $825,720 each payable in full on delivery to our Houston Intercontinental Airport Warehouse 7 loading dock on or about 1 August 2016.
Sincerely,

John T. Smith

Figure WB 5-1. Corporate correspondence.

15. You are the Director of Maintenance for Great Plains Airlines, Inc. You determine that the airline could achieve significant cost savings by contracting its aircraft maintenance out to FAA-certified repair stations that would be legitimate independent contractors, instead of continuing to do the maintenance in-house with corporate employees. Who would you expect to have the authority to make the decision on your recommended change? Why?

Online Research Assignments

As assigned by your instructor, prepare to present in class or post online the following research assignment, including hyperlinks to all online resources relied on:

1. Select a nation other than the U.S.

    a. Identify forms of business organization in that nation that correspond to the U.S. corporation, LLC, and LLP.

    b. Compare and contrast those forms of business from the U.S. corporation, LLC, and LLP forms.

6

AVIATION INSURANCE

Review Questions

1. A real estate brokerage firm specializing in large farm and ranch properties scattered across the rural Midwest and western United States hires you to buy a suitable airplane and set up a flight department to enable the company to transport prospective buyers to view these properties. The company will make its money from real estate sales, and there will be no charge to these customers for the air transportation. You are about to buy the aircraft insurance policy.

    a. What is the appropriate *purpose of use* to cover the proposed operations? Why?

    b. On the *hull* coverage, what risks will you insure against? Why?

    c. What method of valuation will you select for the event of a total loss? Why?

    d. Will a policy containing an FAR violation exclusion clause be acceptable? Why?

    e. The company's bank, which has no prior aircraft financing experience, is willing to finance a portion of the purchase price of the aircraft if (and only if) you can ensure that even if the aircraft is destroyed in an accident, any unpaid balance on the loan will be paid in full. Can you accomplish that through your aircraft insurance even if the circumstances of the accident were such that the insurance company would not have to pay the aircraft owner (such as if the aircraft was being flown by an unqualified pilot at the time of the accident)? If so, describe.

2. You are camped beside your floatplane on the shore of a remote lake in the Alaskan wilderness. A friend who operates the same make and model as yours and knows where your favorite fishing hole is stops by to bring you a copy of a new Airworthiness Directive (AD) that the FAA has just issued against these aircraft. The AD requires that a certain test be performed "before further flight." The equipment needed to perform the test is not portable and the only repair facility in the state with that equipment is located over 500 miles away in Anchorage. Therefore, you will be required to obtain a *special flight permit (ferry permit)* from the FAA in order to legally fly the aircraft from your present location to the repair station where the AD can be complied with.

   a. Do most aircraft insurance policies cover operations under a special flight permit?

   b. What would be the prudent thing to do about your aircraft insurance coverage before taking off from the lake? Why?

3. For each of the following events, indicate whether the event triggers considerations relating to your aircraft insurance policy, and explain why.

   a. The aircraft is to be used for a different purpose than before.

   b. A different pilot will be flying the aircraft.

   c. The aircraft is going to be flown outside the contiguous (lower 48) United States.

   d. You have upgraded the aircraft's avionics, adding significantly to its value.

   e. You are going to fly the aircraft to Santa Fe, New Mexico.

f. You have finally paid off the loan you took to purchase the aircraft.

g. You sell the aircraft.

4. What is *subrogation,* and how can renter pilots be protected against it?

5. While filling out your application for aircraft insurance, you round off your total flight time to the next higher 100 hours. You are issued an aircraft insurance policy based on that application but have an accident that causes extensive damage to the aircraft before you actually accumulate the total number of hours you reported on your application for that insurance policy. Is the insurance company obligated to pay for repair of the aircraft? Explain.

6. While you believe that you have now accumulated over 10,000 hours of flight time, it has been your habit to record in your pilot logbook only time required by FAR to be logged to show proficiency, so you have logged only 3,000 hours of flight time. Which figure should you use in your application for aircraft insurance? Why?

7. Your airplane crashed, and a passenger was injured. You are absolutely certain the accident was not your fault. Does your insurance company have to get your permission to pay a settlement to the injured passenger?

8. You are opening an aircraft repair station that will inspect, repair, and modify customer's aircraft, providing necessary parts in the process. The business has its own hangar, where the work will be performed, and offices including a reception area and pilot lounge for customers along one side of the hangar. The business will not own or operate any aircraft. What insurance coverages will the business need?

9. State the appropriate aircraft insurance *purpose of use* for each of the following operations:
   a. A flight school

   b. An air charter company

   c. An air cargo company

   d. Forest fire fighting

   e. A full-service FBO

   f. A corporate jet

   g. A sport plane for personal recreational acrobatic flying

   h. A sport plane for commercial dual acrobatic instruction

i. A hot-air balloon for personal recreational flying

j. A hot-air balloon for hire for rides

k. A hot-air balloon for commercial bungee jumping

l. Crop spraying

m. A commercial civilian "Introduction to air combat maneuvering" school, using former military aircraft.

10. When you receive your aircraft insurance policy, what should you do with it?

11. Your corporate flight department typically transports very highly paid customers of the company, but your aircraft insurance policy has a liability limit of $100,000 per passenger seat (which wouldn't even begin to cover the probable judgment if even one of these high rollers was killed or injured in the crash of one of your company's aircraft). If you are unable to purchase aircraft insurance with liability limits sufficiently high to cover a typical plane load of non-employee passengers (the company's employee passengers are covered by worker's compensation insurance), is any other insurance available to cover liability above and beyond the aircraft insurance policy's liability limits? If so, describe.

12. Your aircraft insurance company hears a credible rumor that although you are not a licensed aircraft mechanic, you are doing all of the inspections and maintenance on your aircraft, and an accommodating A&P Mechanic with Inspection Authorization is signing off all your work, sight unseen, for a modest fee. You have not yet had an accident, incident, or claim.

   a. What is your aviation insurance company likely to do as a result of receiving this information?

   b. Would this action by your insurance company have any effect on your future ability to purchase aircraft insurance?

13. What effect has the General Aviation Revitalization Act (GARA) had on products liability for aircraft manufacturers, repair stations, and mechanics?

14. You manage the flight department that operates a dozen multimillion-dollar jets transporting executives, guests, and customers for a corporation that does business internationally. One of the nations where the corporation does very lucrative business is experiencing civil unrest characterized by increasingly violent anti-government and anti-western demonstrations. The corporation's legal department is concerned that the corporation's present aircraft insurance policy might not cover the kind of risks that are developing in that nation, since the policy includes Lloyd's form AVN 48B, captioned "War, Hi-jacking, and Other Perils Exclusion Clause." Is there a way to insure this risk? If so, describe.

Online Research Assignments

As assigned by your instructor, prepare to present in class or post online one or more of the following research assignments, including hyperlinks to all online resources relied on:

1. What insurance is now available for commercial operators of unmanned aircraft? Are FAR violation exclusion clauses included in such insurance policies?

2. What insurance is now available for unmanned commercial spaceflight operations?

3. What insurance is now available for manned commercial spaceflight operations, including space tourists such as passengers on Virgin Galactic?

7

EXCULPATORY CONTRACTS

Review Questions

1. What is an *exculpatory contract*?

2. Which affords you better protection from liability losses: an exculpatory contract or adequate liability insurance?

3. You manage an air charter company operating under 14 CFR Part 135. The premium for the liability portion of your aircraft insurance is one of the business's major expenses. Can the company drop that insurance and protect itself by having passengers sign an exculpatory contract instead? Why?

4. Are there any states in which exculpatory contracts are void and unenforceable as a matter of law? If so, where?

5. Can an enforceable exculpatory contract be created by "fine print" on the back of an admission ticket to an air show if the ticket is neither read nor signed by the spectator?

6. You are starting a commercial operation offering suborbital space flights. You find that you cannot buy liability insurance for this operation, at any price. What, if anything, can you do to manage the risk of liability for injury to your wealthy but adventuresome passengers?

7. You are operating a commercial skydiving school. Before jumping, each parachutist is required to sign an exculpatory contract drafted by the school's lawyer. Assume the contract to be legally valid in your state. A jumper experiences a main parachute malfunction and fails to follow the proper sequence of emergency procedures to deploy her reserve parachute, so that it becomes entangled with the malfunctioned main chute. Plummeting to earth at a high rate of speed, the jumper lands on a resident who is mowing his lawn, killing them both.

    a. Will the exculpatory contract protect the skydiving school from a lawsuit by the jumper's spouse claiming that the school negligently trained and supervised the jumper? Explain.

    b. Will the exculpatory contract protect the school against a lawsuit by the spouse of the deceased resident, claiming that the school was negligent in training and supervising the parachutist? Why?

8. You are operating a commercial civilian air combat maneuvering school. Because you have found the cost of aircraft liability insurance for these operations prohibitive, you are having each customer of your $500 "fighter pilot for a day" program sign an exculpatory contract. A sharp, mature, and robust local high school football star has received a gift certificate for your course as a seventeenth-birthday present from his parents.

    a. If he signs your exculpatory contract, will that protect you and your business from a lawsuit in the event that he is injured?

    b. Are there any other measures you can take to strengthen the legal effect of his exculpatory contract?

    c. What will you do, and why?

Online Research Assignments

As assigned by your instructor, prepare to present in class or post online one or more of the following research assignments, including hyperlinks to all online resources relied on:

1. Are participants in Red Bull Air Races required to sign an exculpatory contract? If so, describe in detail or provide a copy of the actual agreement.

2. Are participants in the National Championship Air Races in Reno, Nevada required to sign an exculpatory contract? Does exculpatory language appear on the ticket for spectators admitted to the venue for that event? If "yes" to either question, describe in detail or provide a copy of the actual agreement.

3. Identify an amateur rocketry club or event. Determine whether the club or event requires participants or spectators to sign an exculpatory contract or otherwise relies on exculpatory language to protect the organization and/or others against claims for injuries that may result. If so, describe in detail or provide a copy of the actual agreement or document.

4. For a nation other than the U.S., identify a high-risk aviation or aerospace activity, operation, or event, then determine whether exculpatory contracts, exculpatory language in admission tickets, or similar techniques are used to protect the operator against claims for compensation that might otherwise be made in the event of injury to a participant or spectator. If so, describe in detail or provide a copy of the actual document.

8

AIRLINE LIABILITY

Review Questions

1. From the standpoint of legal liability for negligence, what difference does it make whether a domestic commercial flight is a common-carrier or a contract-carrier operation?

2. Is the *assumption of risk* defense available to an airline to defend against lawsuits brought by injured passengers or the survivors of passengers killed in an airline crash? Why?

3. What is an airline *tariff*? Where would you find it?

4. Can an airline use its tariffs to limit its potential liability to passengers or shippers? If so, describe.

5. Can an airline use its tariffs to limit the airline's liability for passenger injury or death? Why?

6. Can a mixture of domestic and international passengers be on the same flight?

7. How can you tell whether a person is a domestic or an international passenger? Describe.

8. What treaty is *now* the primary source of law governing the legal relationship between airlines and their international passengers?

9. It is a snowy and bitterly cold winter day in Cleveland when the commuter airline flight from Montreal, Canada, pulls up to the gate. As the international passengers are walking across the ramp from the airliner to the terminal building, one of them slips on an icy patch and suffers an injury. Is the airline liable for this passenger's injury? Why? Are there any artificial dollar limits on that liability?

10. If in the previous question the flight came from Chicago and the passenger who fell was a domestic passenger, under what circumstances and to what extent would the airline be liable for that passenger's injury?

11. A domestic passenger and an international passenger are standing side by side in the airline terminal's baggage claim area waiting for their bags to arrive when a lone terrorist walks up and detonates his suicide vest, killing them both. Is the airline liable for either death? Explain.

12. What effect does the Montreal Convention have on the legal liability of anyone other than the airline (for example, the aircraft's manufacturer, air traffic controllers, or the airport owner/operator) for the death or injury of an international airline passenger?

13. Snow Bird Airlines flight 13 provides nonstop service between Anchorage and Phoenix. All passengers aboard today's flight are ticketed from Anchorage to Phoenix and none has an origin or destination in another country on his or her ticket. A pressurization problem arises en route, and the crew decides to make a precautionary landing in Vancouver, Canada. If this attempted stop in Canada leads to an accident, will the Montreal Convention apply? Why?

14. Aero Cargo flight 13 provides nonstop cargo service between Bogota, Columbia and Miami. Prior to takeoff from Bogota, the crew is unable to start one of the engines on the aging four-engine DC-7C. Advised of the problem, the company's chief pilot and vice president of operations orders the crew to proceed on schedule with the cargo using the three functioning engines (a procedure known in the company as "attempting an air start"), making it clear that if the pilots do not comply, they will be fired. The pilots attempt the takeoff, but the aircraft is not airborne at the end of the runway, where it crashes and burns. What is the airline's liability, if any, for the resulting destruction of the cargo if both the United States and Columbia have ratified the Montreal Convention?

15. What effect has ratification of the Montreal Convention had on the volume of litigation of claims for injury to international airline passengers?

16. Why did the United States not experience an explosion in civil litigation arising out of the deaths of thousands of people from the terrorist attacks using hijacked airliners on 9/11/01?

Online Research Assignments

As assigned by your instructor, prepare to present in class or post online the following research assignment, including hyperlinks to all online resources relied on:

1. Select an airline crash that occurred on an international flight within the last 10 years. For that crash, identify the applicable governing international agreement(s), then analyze the airline's legal liability for:

    i.   Passenger injuries (including death)

    ii. Damage to cargo

    iii. Punitive or exemplary damages

    iv. Damage to persons and/or property on the ground, if any

GOVERNMENT LIABILITY

Review Questions

1. Compare and contrast the vicarious liability of the federal government for the consequences of torts committed by its employees with the same liability of employers in the private sector.

2. Compare and contrast the personal liability for the consequences of torts committed by individual federal employees with that of individual employees in the private sector.

3. Your best friend from college was in ROTC and on graduation was commissioned as an officer and trained as a fighter pilot. Your friend experienced an engine failure on takeoff from an air base in Afghanistan and was killed when the aircraft's ejection seat failed to function. Your friend's spouse, who is very worried about how to support the couple's two young children, asks whether you think they might be able to successfully sue the federal government or anybody else for your friend's death. Analyze the potential legal liabilities for each of the following causation scenarios, showing your reasoning:

   a. The ejection seat failure was determined to have been caused by a design defect incorporated in the specifications provided to the manufacturer by the United States.

   b. The failure was determined to have been caused by an assembly line worker in the ejection seat manufacturer's plant, who assembled the trigger mechanism incorrectly.

4. You are an air traffic controller employed by the FAA. An aircraft crashes in your operational sector, and an attorney for persons injured in the crash sues you personally for negligence, claiming that the instructions you gave the pilot caused the crash. Will the U.S. Attorney help you? How?

5. What is a *discretionary function*? What other kind of exercise of judgment is there? Distinguish.

6. What difference does it make whether a government employee's activities alleged to have contributed to cause an aircraft accident were a discretionary function or not?

7. A midair collision occurs within the Class D airspace of a local airport that has a control tower operated by the FAA. Visibility at the time of the accident was three miles (marginal VMC), and both aircraft had radioed the tower a minute or two before the collision, reporting similar positions. Each obtained landing instructions and the tower warned the second aircraft that another aircraft had reported inbound from the same area. The aircraft were not yet visible to the tower controllers when the collision occurred. One of the distraught tower controllers later lamented to the news media: "I told Washington months ago that we needed radar at this tower and that if we didn't get it pretty soon, there was probably going to be a midair collision. If only we'd had radar, we could have kept those planes apart." Can the survivors of the people who died in the collision reasonably hope to successfully sue the federal government for the FAA's negligence in not installing air traffic radar at this airport? Explain.

8. During night operations under VMC at a busy major airline hub having a control tower operated by the FAA, the local controller clears a regional airliner to line up and wait preparatory to take off on runway 26R. The regional airline crew properly acknowledges the clearance and moves onto the runway, halting in position for takeoff. Distracted, the local controller then forgets about the regional airliner and clears a jumbo jet to land on the same runway. The larger airliner lands on top of the waiting regional airliner. Both aircraft are substantially destroyed by the collision and ensuing fire, and there are numerous passenger and crewmember deaths and injuries.

   a. Who is potentially liable, and why?

   b. If more than one person or entity is found legally liable, how will the responsibility to pay the plaintiff's damages be apportioned? Describe.

9. Is the United States liable for negligence of a FAA Designee, such as an AME, DAR, DER, DMR, IA, or ODA?

10. An air traffic controller is going through a bitter divorce. One dark and stormy night the controller realizes that among the aircraft he's controlling is a private jet owned by the man who stole the affection of his soon-to-be-former spouse, and that she is among the passengers in that aircraft. In a fit of anger and jealous rage, the controller deliberately gives the jet a series of vectors to the final approach course intended to confuse the crew's situational awareness before putting them on a course at an assigned altitude that causes the aircraft to collide with an obstacle. There are no survivors. Will the U.S. be held liable for the controller's actions?

Online Research Assignments

As assigned by your instructor, prepare to present in class or post online one or more of the following research assignments, including hyperlinks to all online resources relied on:

1. Has FAA policy on the delegation of some certification authority over commercial transport aircraft to manufacturers under organization designation authorizations (ODA) changed as a result of the Lion Air and Ethiopian Airlines disaster investigations? If so, describe.

2. For a nation other than the U.S., identify the law(s) governing the liability of the government and government employees for injuries caused by negligence in:

   a. Air traffic control,

   b. Aviation weather reporting, and

   c. Aircraft airworthiness certification.

10

ACCIDENT NOTIFICATION, REPORTING AND INVESTIGATION

Review Questions

1. While attempting to land a single-engine tailwheel airplane in a crosswind at a private uncontrolled airfield, you lost control and the aircraft "ground-looped."

   a. The right wingtip was damaged to the extent that it will have to be repaired or replaced before further flight. Are you required to notify any government agency of this event? Explain.

   b. During the course of the ground loop, the right main landing gear leg also failed. Now are you required to notify any government agency of this event? Explain.

   c. When the landing gear failed, the propeller struck the ground and was bent. Now are you required to notify any government agency of this event? Explain. If the ground impact caused a propeller blade to separate from the aircraft would you arrive at the same or a different answer? Explain.

   d. A subsequent tear-down inspection of the engine reveals that the prop strike bent the crankshaft. Now are you required to notify any government agency of the event? Explain.

e. During the landing events, your head was banged against the aircraft's structure. Although you did not lose consciousness, you experienced an extreme headache and dizziness and were hospitalized for treatment for a concussion. Now are you required to notify any government agency of this event? Explain.

2. You just landed a light twin without first lowering the landing gear. Both propellers are curled back, the flaps are bent, and there are some dents and scrapes on the aircraft's belly skin.

    a. You believe the cause was that you were distracted in your performance of the aircraft's prelanding checklist by the air traffic controller calling to point out other traffic to you. Are you required to notify any government agency about this mishap? Explain.

    b. You believe that the cause was a malfunction or failure of the landing gear system, because you remember placing the gear handle in the "down" position and observing three illuminated green lights, indicating that all three landing gear were down and locked. Are you required to notify any government agency of this mishap? Explain.

    c. A tear-down inspection of the engines reveals that both crankshafts were bent when the propellers struck the ground. Now are you required to notify any government agency of this event? Explain.

3. While operating at an uncontrolled airport, you have a midair collision with another aircraft that you did not see and that had no radio with which to report its whereabouts or intentions.

    a. Fortunately for everyone involved, your aircraft suffered no damage, and the only damage to the other aircraft was a small hole punctured in the upper skin of a wing by your landing gear. No one was hurt, and both aircraft landed uneventfully. Are you required to notify any government agency of this mishap? Explain.

b. The two aircraft involved were both blimps, which merely bounced off each other rather comically, with no damage to either aircraft. Are you required to notify any government agency of this mishap? Explain.

c. The two aircraft did not collide, but missed each other by no more than a millimeter. Are you required to notify any government agency of this event? Explain.

4. You are flying a large jet transport and experience a failure of one of the four turbine engines. No one is injured, and you are able to make a successful emergency landing.

a. The failure was apparently caused by ingesting a large bird, which caused numerous turbine blades to break off and be blown out the engine exhaust. Are you required to notify any government agency of this occurrence? Explain.

b. The failure was catastrophic and uncontained, causing a turbine wheel to emerge from the side of the engine cowling, penetrating and lodging in the fuselage. Now are you required to notify any government agency of this occurrence? Explain.

5. You are operating an aircraft equipped with a single electronic primary flight display. While in flight the screen goes dark, displaying no information. You have no other electronic cockpit displays. Are you required to notify any government agency of this failure? Does your answer depend upon whether you are operating in IMC or VMC at the time? Explain.

6. While maneuvering on an aircraft parking ramp, a line service attendant accidentally strikes a parked and unoccupied helicopter's main rotor blade with the gas truck, damaging it to the extent that the blade will have to be replaced. Must any government agency be notified of this mishap? Explain.

7. You are operating a regional airliner. On takeoff roll, you observe a small general aviation aircraft beginning to cross your runway ahead. You apply full braking and full reverse thrust, successfully aborting the takeoff and stopping short of the other aircraft. Are you required to notify any government agency of this occurrence? Explain.

8. What accidents and incidents are you required to report to the FAA?

9. Flying your personal single-engine airplane non-commercially, you experience an in-flight engine failure and make an emergency landing on a freeway below.

   a. You land and roll off into the median without damage to the aircraft or anything else. There are no injuries. Are you required to notify any government agency of this event? Explain.

   b. You land on and destroy a $200,000 exotic sports car. Seeing the aircraft coming, the car's occupants jump out and escape unscathed, and there is no damage to the aircraft except some scraped paint and a flat tire. The occupants of the aircraft are not injured. Are you required to notify any government agency of this occurrence? Explain.

10. A catering truck rolls into a parked airliner, damaging the fuselage and pressure vessel to the extent that it will require a major repair before flight.

    a. Only the aircraft cleaning crew is aboard at the time of the collision. Is the airline required to notify any government agency of this occurrence? Explain.

    b. The passengers have not yet begun to board the aircraft at the time of the collision, but the flight crew is aboard preparing the aircraft for departure when the collision occurs. Is the airline required to notify any government agency of this occurrence? Explain.

11. You are involved in an accident as a flight crewmember. During the on-site phase of the accident investigation, the NTSB wants to ask you some questions. The accident investigation team includes some FAA personnel.

   a. If you make a statement in the presence of these FAA personnel, can it be used against you in an enforcement action?

   b. Is there a way to cooperate with the NTSB at this point by discussing the accident with them, without running the risk of giving the FAA ammunition to suspend or revoke your certificate in a subsequent enforcement case? If so, describe.

12. You just walked away from a spectacular crash that totally destroyed the airplane. You have walked only a few yards when someone who obviously saw the crash comes running up to you and says: "I can't believe you're alive. What happened?" You're pretty sure that you forgot to disengage the gust locks on the aircraft's control surfaces before attempting to take off.

   a. What will you say and why?

   b. Who must you notify about this accident, and when and how?

   c. To whom are you required to submit a written report about the accident, and when?

13. What support services does the NTSB make available to families of airline disaster victims?

14. Landing at an unfamiliar airport at the conclusion of a charter flight, the crew of a business jet inadvertently lands on a taxiway parallel to the runway assigned by ATC. The landing is successful and there is no conflict with other traffic. Is the operator required to notify the NTSB of the mistake? Is the operator required to file a written report of the event with the NTSB? Explain.

15. If the flight in Question 14 is not a charter but a non-commercial corporate flight department operation, is the operator required to notify the NTSB of the mistake? Is the operator required to file a written report of the event with the NTSB? Explain.

Online Research Assignments

As assigned by your instructor, prepare to present in class or post online one or more of the following research assignments, including hyperlinks to all online resources relied on:

1. Determine whether any changes have been made to NTSB Part 830 since January 2020.

2. Determine whether U.S. law has assigned responsibility for investigation and determination of the probable cause of commercial spacecraft accidents to a specific federal agency and, if not, whether a Bill proposing such legislation has been introduced in Congress and, if so, its status.

3. For a nation or union of nations other than the U.S., identify the government entity or entities responsible for investigation of civil aircraft accidents and for determination of the probable cause of such accidents. Compare and contrast civil aircraft accident notification and reporting requirements in that nation with those of the U.S. described in this chapter.

4. For a spacefaring nation or union of nations other than the U.S., determine whether responsibility for investigation and determination of the probable cause of commercial spacecraft accidents has been assigned to a specific governmental entity.

PART III

Aircraft Transactions

11

BUYING AND SELLING AIRCRAFT

Review Questions

1. What is a *security interest*?

2. What right does the holder of a security interest have that other creditors do not?

3. Will a title search at the FAA Aircraft Registry in Oklahoma City reveal *all* kinds of valid security interests in aircraft?

4. You are the manager of an FBO. A customer purchases a new airplane through your business. A bank finances that purchase, obtains a security interest in the aircraft through a written security agreement signed by the purchaser, and files that security agreement with the FAA Aircraft Registry and the International Registry. Later, the customer has your shop install upgraded avionics, including a full "glass cockpit" set of multifunction displays (MFD) integrating flight, navigation, engine, and sensor data.

    a. Do you have the right to require the customer to pay the bill for the equipment and installation in full before you release the aircraft back to the customer? Explain.

b. If the aircraft owner went bankrupt at that point (when the work has been done, the bill has not been paid, and the FBO still has the aircraft), who will be paid first from the sale of the aircraft, the FBO or the bank? Why?

c. In initial discussions over the price of the equipment and installation, the customer indicates that she wants to buy the unit and have your shop install it, but she would like to pay the price for the equipment and installation in three equal monthly payments, rather than all at once. This is acceptable to you. Is there anything you can require as a condition of releasing the aircraft back to its owner before the debt is paid in full to protect the FBO's security interest in the aircraft for this installation? If so, describe.

d. After the transaction described in c. above, your shop installs the equipment in the aircraft and releases it to the owner. Before the bill is paid, the aircraft owner files bankruptcy. Now who is in the superior position to be paid first out of the proceeds of the sale of the aircraft: the FBO or the bank? Explain.

5. You are an aircraft broker specializing in airline-size jets. A customer contacts you, indicating that he is the chief executive officer of an international cattle-breeding operation based in Texas. He advises you that neither he nor anyone on his staff knows much about large airplanes, but they need to purchase an aircraft capable of transporting 100 bulls weighing an average of 1,600 pounds each, each in a 150-pound shipping cage measuring 5 feet wide by 8 feet long by 6 feet high. He states that the aircraft will also need to be capable of carrying that load from Dallas to Buenos Aires, Argentina, nonstop. If you sell an aircraft to this customer for that purpose, what warranties will you be making to the buyer?

6. You are a co-owner of a business that has a dealership for a major manufacturer of general aviation aircraft. The aircraft typically arrive at your dealership from the factory ready for delivery to the customer, and your company does not usually perform any inspection or other work on the aircraft prior to sale and delivery to a buyer. A new aircraft your company recently sold to a customer has crashed, killing everyone aboard. It appears that the crash was caused by a design or manufacturing defect.

   a. Is your business exposed to any risk of being found liable? Explain.

   b. If such liability is found, will it make any difference to you whether your company was organized as a partnership or a corporation? Explain.

Online Research Assignments

As assigned by your instructor, prepare to present in class or post online one or more of the following research assignments, including hyperlinks to all online resources relied on:

1. For a nation other than the U.S., identify the government entity that is the counterpart of the FAA Aircraft Registry. Civil aircraft registered in the U.S. are identified by the letter N, followed by numbers or a combination of numbers and letters. What markings identify civil aircraft registered in the nation you chose?

2. Has the FAA imposed a requirement to register any class of civil unmanned aircraft with the FAA Aircraft Registry? If so, describe.

3. For a nation other than the U.S., has the government imposed a requirement to register any class of civil unmanned aircraft with the appropriate civil aviation authority? If so, describe.

4. For a nation or union of nations other than the U.S., determine if there is a counterpart to the Uniform Commercial Code. If so, compare and contrast its provisions relating to security interests and warranties to those of the UCC.

12

AIRCRAFT LEASING, CO-OWNERSHIP AND FRACTIONAL OWNERSHIP

Review Questions

1. What is the difference between a *lease* and a *leaseback*?

2. Distinguish the primary motivation of the lessee in a lease ("lease forward") from that of the seller-lessee in a sale with leaseback.

3. Explain how that difference in primary motivations may lead the seller-lessee in a leaseback to act in a manner that may be contrary to the owner-lessor's best interests.

4. You are an aircraft owner and hold a commercial pilot certificate, but do not hold a Part 135 certificate. Can you legally rent or lease your aircraft to others and then allow them to hire you as their personal pilot to fly the aircraft for them in their travels? Explain.

5. How can you save money on attorney fees in the drafting of an aircraft lease?

6. You own an aircraft. A person you have seen around the airport but don't know very well approaches you with a business proposition. She informs you that she is starting a commercial flying club and would like to lease your aircraft. What will you do to decide whether you want to do business with this person?

7. You are approached by a pilot who says he owns the same make and model of general aviation aircraft as yours. He says that his annual inspection is taking longer than expected, interfering with his family's long-scheduled vacation plans. He asks to lease your aircraft for their planned two-week family vacation trip. He offers you a good price and even offers to pay cash in advance. You have had some major unexpected family expenses and could really use the money, but you are left with the uneasy feeling that a family vacation may not really be what the pilot intends. If you decide to just take the money and not ask any pointed questions or otherwise check this person out, are you running any special risks? Explain.

8. You have been using your aircraft only for your own personal business and pleasure flying. To produce some income, you decide to lease it to an FBO that will use it for student instruction and rental. Will this require any changes in your aircraft insurance coverage? If so, describe.

9. What is *fractional ownership*?

10. What advantages do fractional ownership programs offer air travelers as compared to chartering or purchasing similar aircraft as sole owners?

11. What legal documents are necessary components of a fractional ownership program?

12. What users will find fractional ownership more economical than either charter or outright sole ownership of an aircraft?

Online Research Assignments

As assigned by your instructor, prepare to present in class or post online one or both of the following research assignments, including hyperlinks to all online resources relied on:

1. For ground transportation, ride-sharing programs such as Uber are gaining popularity. Several companies, such as OpenAirplane, DiamondShare, AirPower, Flytenow and SkyPool were formed to offer similar air transportation programs using privately owned, non-commercially operated aircraft on an expense-sharing basis under 14 CFR § 61.113(b). Determine the FAA's present position on the legality of such operations and the reasoning behind that position, and then evaluate its reasonableness.

2. For a nation or union of nations other than the U.S., determine whether any civil aviation ride-sharing programs are operating and the position of the appropriate civil aviation regulatory authority on their legality. If any are operating, briefly describe the program and the extent of its success.

PART IV

Airports, Airspace,
and Aviation Security

13

AIRPORTS AND TERMINAL AIRSPACE

Review Questions

1. What two areas of concern have been the focus of most litigation regarding airports and airspace?

2. What is the power of *eminent domain*?

3. How does a government normally exercise its power of eminent domain?

4. What is *inverse condemnation*?

5. If a government takes private property under its power of eminent domain, is it required to pay for it? If so, how much?

6. Describe two common uses of the power of eminent domain to solve the legal problems identified in your answer to Question 1, above.

7. What is the *police power*?

8. Describe two common uses of the police power to solve the legal problems identified in your answer to Question 1, above.

9. Can a government's exercise of its police power ever lead to a situation in which the government would be required to pay compensation to a private landowner?

10. What are the sources of the FAA's authority to regulate airspace use and flight safety?

11. If a state, county, or city government adopts a law governing aviation that conflicts with federal law, will that state or local law be enforceable? Why?

12. Can state and local governments regulate flight operations? Explain.

13. You own and operate a private airport that is open to the public. Does the power of eminent domain allow you to condemn aviation easements over your neighbor's property for the use of aircraft coming and going from your airport? Explain.

14. Can a city or county government prohibit you from using your own private property as an airport or heliport? Explain.

15. If you own a private airport, what limitations can you impose on use of the airport by others?

16. You are the airport manager of a city-owned public airport. The airport's development has been partially funded through federal grants. The airport authority, your boss, asks you the following questions:

    a. Is there any restriction on what limitations we can impose on the use of our airport?

    b. Would there be any potential adverse legal consequences if we decide to close the airport and use the property for other purposes?

17. A regional airport authority has been formed to design, build, and operate a new public air carrier airport, and you have been hired as a consultant to the authority. It is anticipated that if you do a good job, you will be offered the position of airport manager once the facility opens. The project right now is something of a political "hot potato," and it seems that there are many public concerns about the costs and consequences of the project. The authority has set up a public hearing to afford citizens and the news media the opportunity to ask whatever questions they may have about the project to allay their fears and correct their misconceptions. You will be on the panel responding to them and must be prepared to answer questions in the following areas:

    a. Are any federal matching funds available to help pay the costs for planning and construction of the new airport, and if so, what is the name of that program and what is the maximum percentage of the total project costs that can be funded by it?

    b. What, if anything, can be done to prevent private developers from putting up hotels, office buildings, apartment houses, or condominiums on adjacent private property that could obstruct aircraft coming and going from the airport after all this money has been spent on airport development?

    c. What can be done to control the noise of aircraft using the airport?

d. The future airport site is in an undeveloped rural area. What can be done to keep private developers from building homes and other noise-sensitive projects in areas that will be most heavily impacted by noise from aircraft using the airport, and to otherwise buffer future residential developments from airport noise?

18. You own a horse ranch. A regional airport authority builds a jetport nearby with runways oriented so that aircraft taking off and landing at the airport frighten and stampede your horses. Several of your most valuable thoroughbreds have been badly injured crashing into fences when panicked by the aircraft, and your family can't even get a good night's sleep anymore because of the noise from the jets.

a. Can you get an injunction to make them stop flying so low over your ranch? Explain.

b. Do you have any legal recourse for this problem? Explain.

19. You have just moved into a new house in the country. At first light, your sleep is disturbed by loud engine noises and voices. Peering out the window, you see on the property adjacent to yours a crew loading a crop-spraying aircraft, which takes off, sprays an insecticide on a nearby field, and returns for reloading. This continues throughout the morning. When you inquire about what is going on, the crew advises you that the land is zoned as a private airport, and that the operation has been in business in this location for over 50 years, and that they "ain't going no place." They further advise you that this is the first day of their crop-spraying season and you can expect this activity every day from first light until last light, weather permitting, until mid-October.

a. Do you have any legal recourse against the airport operator? Explain.

b. Your new house is one of many in a large new subdivision adjacent to this airport. The aerial applicator who owns the airport would rather not engage the adjacent landowners in a long and expensive legal battle with uncertain consequences. What might the aerial applicator consider doing to alleviate conflict with the neighbors?

c. The entire area in the vicinity of this airfield has become prime real estate for residential development. How may this affect the aerial applicator's ability to remain in operation at this location? Explain.

20. You are the airport manager of a city-owned public airport. The airport's development has been partially funded through federal grants. There is only one FBO on the airport, a business that has been there since the airport opened and that enjoys a very close, even cozy, relationship with the airport authority. Someone else proposes to open a second FBO at the airport. The airport authority is concerned that there is not enough business to support two FBOs, and wishes to protect the established FBO that has served the airport for so long.

    a. Can the city legally impose a policy that will not permit establishment of a second FBO under any circumstances? Why?

    b. If the city imposes such a policy, what recourse is available to the proponent of the second FBO?

    c. There is only one car rental agency at the airport. It has also been on the airport for a long time and the airport authority feels very protective toward its owners. Someone applies for permission to open a competing car rental agency on the airport. Would it be a violation of the airport's federal grant agreement for the airport authority to prohibit a second car rental agency on the airport? Explain.

21. How long is an airport operator bound by the restrictions of the grant agreement if federal airport development funds are accepted?

22. Is an environmental impact study required to be completed before an airport improvement project or construction of a new airport can commence?

23. Your aircraft is hangared at a popular general aviation airport owned and operated by the city you live in. In fact, you chose to buy a home in that city precisely because it was so convenient to this airport. The airport has been developed with the help of federal matching funds. The most recent federal Airport Improvement Program grant was received by the city five years ago, to enable extension and resurfacing of the main runway. You have just learned that the city has announced plans to close the airport and sell the property to a developer who plans to build a commercial energy-producing wind generator farm on the site. Can you and other pilots who use the airport successfully sue in court to block the closure, based on promises the city made to the FAA as part of the last grant agreement? Why?

Online Research Assignments

As assigned by your instructor, prepare to present in class or post online the following research assignment, including hyperlinks to all online resources relied on:

1. For a civil airport of your choice, located anywhere in the world, determine what steps (if any) have been taken to:

   a. Protect the surrounding airspace from obstruction by obstacles.

   b. Assure that land uses surrounding the airport are compatible with aircraft noise.

   c. Tailor runway-use preferences, along with approach and departure paths, to minimize noise over surrounding areas.

   d. Identify the legal power or powers used to accomplish each of those steps, and

   e. Provide images illustrating the airport and vicinity and each of the steps taken to address the topics above.

   f. Identify current airport noise and safety issues that remain of concern to the community and current activity to address those issues.

2. Describe the current status of:

   a. the Paris Agreement and implementing or superseding international treaties and agreements affecting civil aviation GHG emissions, and

   b. the CORSIA agreement for international airline emissions.

14

FAA REGULATION OF AIRSPACE

Review Questions

1. Who is empowered to regulate the use of navigable airspace over the U.S.?

2. The National Park Service (NPS) of the U.S. Department of Interior desires regulatory changes to reduce the aircraft noise level in Denali National Park, Alaska. Can the NPS legally:

   a. Prohibit aircraft from flying over certain areas of the park and fine violators? Why?

   b. Impose noise limits on aircraft flying over the park and fine violators? Why?

   c. Prohibit aircraft from landing and taking off from locations within the park, such as the Kahiltna Glacier, a popular spot used by ski-equipped airplanes to drop off and pick up climbers assaulting the peak of Denali? Why?

   d. Impose noise limits on aircraft landing and taking off from Kahiltna Glacier? Why?

3. The U.S. Navy wishes to exclude civil aircraft from certain airspace along Virginia's Atlantic coast (now designated as an MOA) in order to use the airspace for air combat maneuvering practice without participating pilots having to keep a sharp lookout for transient civilian air traffic.

    a. Can the Navy simply declare that airspace off limits to civil aircraft? Why?

    b. Identify the first legal procedural step the Navy must take to obtain the desired change to this airspace designation.

    c. Describe the legal procedural steps that must follow to assure that interested parties are aware of the proposed change and have a reasonable opportunity to express their views on the subject.

4. Flying at 3,500 feet MSL over the Arctic National Wildlife Refuge in Alaska, you observe a huge herd of migrating caribou. Your passenger, a very generous tourist, asks you to descend so he can record the spectacle on video. He promises you a nice tip if you'll grant his request, and indicates that the lower you go, the bigger your bonus will be. What will you do and why?

5. As an aircraft owner and private pilot, as well as a sailing aficionado, you always like to fly over (always at a safe altitude and distance) with your closest friends as passengers to observe the annual sailing regatta put on by a local yacht club in an area under Class G (uncontrolled) airspace. The event comes around again tomorrow, and you and your passengers are especially excited, because the nightly news just reported that the president of the United States will be a participant in this year's event. Could this affect your plans? Why?

Online Research Assignments

As assigned by your instructor, prepare to present in class or post online one or more of the following research assignments, including hyperlinks to all online resources relied on:

1. For areas of armed conflict:

   a. Determine authority, methods, policies and procedures in current use to warn civil aircraft of threats to safe passage and assist in avoidance of those threats.

   b. Evaluate the efficacy of those in current practices.

   c. Identify proposed changes to the current practices and evaluate the pros and cons of those proposals.

2. For airspace over international waters:

   a. Determine the role of ICAO and the controlling authority, if any, for airspace and air traffic tracking and control over international waters in one of the following areas:

      i.   North Atlantic

      ii. South Atlantic

      iii. North Pacific

      iv. South Pacific

      v.   Indian Ocean

      vi. Arctic Ocean

   b. For that area, describe any shortcomings that have been identified in present practices.

   c. Identify proposed changes to current practices and evaluate the pros and cons of each.

3. For a nation or union of nations other than the U.S.:

   a. Identify the government agency or agencies charged with regulating the airspace and controlling air traffic.

   b. Compare and contrast the airspace categories with those of the U.S. described in this chapter.

   c. Compare and contrast procedures for changing airspace categorizations with the procedures prescribed in the U.S. Administrative Procedure Act.

   d. Describe proposed changes to a. and b. under discussion and evaluate the pros and cons of each.

4. Identify current challenges and efforts to accomplish the safe and efficient integration of civil unmanned aircraft into:

   a. The U.S. National Airspace System or,

   b. International airspace over the high seas or,

   c. The airspace of nation or union of nations other than the U.S.

15

CRIMES, CIVIL OFFENSES, AND AVIATION SECURITY

Review Questions

1. You are a member of a flying club. One morning at the clubhouse, you overhear a conversation between a couple of the club's pilots who are about to go flying. You know the pair to be VFR-only pilots who don't file flight plans because they believe it's none of the government's business where they're flying. The two are mad that the FAA, citing reasons of national security, has recently established a Prohibited Area over a nearby nuclear power plant. Combined with existing Class B and Special Use airspace in the area, circumnavigating the new Prohibited Area will require them to deviate from the customary and preferred direct route to and from their destination, adding time and expense for the flight. "Here's what we'll do," one of them says, "We'll use this duct tape to change the one in the N-number to look like a 4, then we'll just fly on through the usual way. Hell, they ain't going to shoot us down, and even if they get our N-number, they'll be looking for the wrong airplane." If they do that, will they be risking criminal prosecution in addition to FAA enforcement action? Explain fully.

2. Acting on a tip, law enforcement officers in a major U.S. city take into custody a person believed to be one of the perpetrators of the massacre at Lod International Airport in Israel. Does the U.S. have jurisdiction to try the suspect in U.S. courts for this crime? Explain.

3. A group of homeowners living near a small general aviation airport have worked themselves up into a frenzy over the noise from an aerobatic academy based at the airport. At a homeowners association meeting, one of the members says: "This is war. If those damn

pilots want to make our lives miserable, we can make theirs miserable too. There's not even a fence around that airport. You can walk right up to one of those planes anytime, day or night. I'll bet that if they started having problems with flat tires and scratched paint or busted stuff, they'd move somewhere else." If the speaker or anyone else decides to follow through on the idea, what consequences do they risk? Explain.

4. A group of local pilots are discussing airport security. One of them expresses the opinion that airline security at the local airport is as big a joke as it was before 9/11. "It's those same morons who couldn't get a job flipping burgers, doing the same job they did before, only in different uniforms," he says. "Plus, the whole program assumes that a terrorist is just going to get in line and go through security screening like everybody else. It would be a piece of cake for a terrorist to put on a pair of blue coveralls like the ramp workers wear, slide in through that bent-up old gate down by the old hangar and walk right on to an airliner without anybody challenging him. Fred, why don't you get your video camera and let's go over there and do that and get it on videotape. We'll give the tape to the TV station, and when they show that on the news, somebody will have to get serious about security at the airport."

   a. At this point, has a crime been committed? Explain.

   b. The group agrees to execute the plan. At this point, has a crime been committed? Explain.

   c. Fred goes home, gets his video camera and blue coveralls, and meets some of the others at that old gate. At this point, have any crimes been committed? Explain.

   d. While Fred was gone to get his video camera, another member of the group telephoned the TV station and spoke to investigative reporter Rex, telling him about their plan. Rex expressed the opinion that it was a wonderful idea, enthusiastically encouraged them to go ahead with it, and promised to broadcast their video in a news special on problems with airport security. Has Rex committed any crimes? Explain.

e. Arnold, one of the group engaged in the original conversation fails to show up at the gate, but the others don their blue coveralls and start squeezing one-by-one through the bent gate. The police arrive and arrest them. What crimes, if any, can Arnold be charged with? What additional crimes can the others now be charged with?

f. Instead, the group is not intercepted and completes the mission as planned, without interference. What additional crimes can be charged?

5. You are an airline passenger. As you are approaching the pre-boarding security screening area, you remember that the pocketknife your late grandfather gave you when you were a kid is in the backpack you're carrying with you. If you miss the flight, you'll miss an important job interview. But you really loved your grandfather and that little old knife is precious to you, so you don't want the screeners to take it because you know you'd never get it back. The screeners don't look very organized, so you figure there's a pretty good chance they'll overlook it. What are your options? What will you do and why?

6. A young computer hacker has figured out how to hack into the airport's computer-controlled runway and approach lighting system. He decides to show what incompetent jerks the airport's IT workers are by taking control of the system and turning off the lights from time to time when aircraft are approaching to land at night. Assuming no accident results, could this mischief lead to criminal charges? Explain.

7. An airline passenger is stuck in traffic on her way to the airport. Fearing that she'll miss her flight, it occurs to her that maybe if the airline got an anonymous threat of a bomb on the flight, that would delay the departure long enough for her to catch the flight. What is her downside risk if she decides to make such a call? Explain.

8. You are an auto mechanic by profession and own an airplane that is certified under a standard category airworthiness certificate. You desire to install an auxiliary fuel tank in the aircraft to enable you to fly nonstop to visit your kids at college, but were stunned by your FBO's quoted price to obtain a certified tank and install it for you under an FAA Form 337. You have a fuel tank that's the right size, although it isn't FAA certified, and you know enough about fuel systems to install it and make it work. What are the possible legal consequences if you succeed?

9. You are an airline passenger. During pre-boarding screening, a very annoying TSA employee asks you to open your wallet.

    a. Is this a reasonable search? Why?

    b. Your immediate urge is to respond sarcastically, saying something like: "Oh, darn, that's where I hid the machine gun I was going to use to hijack the flight." What adverse legal consequences could result from such a remark?

10. You have bought a prosperous aircraft repair station from its previous owner, continuing the operation with the same employees. One day in the shop you observe one of your mechanics remove a data plate from an alternator and replace it with another one he removes from a drawer on his work table. When you ask what he's doing, he explains that they purchase alternators from a local discount auto supply shop, then replace the data plate with one showing the unit to be an FAA-approved part. He says the previous owner told them everybody knew the units were identical, but the manufacturer just charged ten times as much for a unit with the FAA-approved data plate. The shop buys them cheap, but charges the customer the manufacturer's list price for the FAA-approved version. He says they've always done that with a lot of parts, which is why the business is so lucrative.

    a. Assuming that the parts are in fact identical except for the data plate, is this action a crime? Explain.

b. Now that you know about the practice, would you be committing a crime if you allow it to continue, as long as you don't do any of the data plate switching yourself? Explain.

c. If the data plate switching is a crime, what are the penalties:

    i. If the part is installed on an aircraft, and works OK?

    ii. If the part is installed on an aircraft and fails because of a difference between the automotive and FAA-approved aircraft versions?

    iii. If the failure of the part causes a fatal accident?

    iv. To your business, for violations past and future?

11. A construction worker has been away from home doing commercial blasting. When he finishes a job, he realizes that he has a case of dynamite left over that isn't accounted for. He could really use that to blow some stumps on his farm when he gets home, but he obviously can't take it with him on the airline. He considers shipping it via air freight, declaring it as household goods. What are the possible adverse consequences of such an act? Explain.

12. At a general aviation airport, you and your co-owner are in your hangar polishing your airplane. Your suspicions are aroused when you notice a person neither of you has ever previously seen around the airport moving down the ramp and peering into parked aircraft. When you see him try to open the door to one, you decide you have to take action. You have a pistol in your car. What will you do, and why?

13. You're an airline passenger having the worst trip of your life. You've experienced delayed and cancelled flights, been slammed around in severe turbulence and puked on by another passenger, the airline has lost your bag, and now a snotty flight attendant is refusing to serve you another drink.

    a. You feel like grabbing the flight attendant by the throat and emphatically explaining that you have reached your breaking point and it is absolutely necessary that you receive another drink right now to calm you down. Would this action be a crime? Explain.

    b. If you went ahead with the action contemplated in a., above, and for further emphasis threatened to strangle the flight attendant to death on the spot unless you got that drink, would this make matters worse for you legally? Explain.

14. A uniformed law enforcement officer working in the terminal building of an airline airport, outside the secured area, notices two men who appear Middle Eastern entering a crowded airport restaurant. Both are carrying suitcases. As they pass close by him, they are conversing softly but excitedly in a language he thinks might be Arabic. They do not make eye contact with him. Can the officer legally:

    a. Stop the pair and question them? Explain.

    b. Frisk them for weapons? Explain.

    c. Search their bags for explosives? Explain.

15. You live near a local airport, and your neighbor has repeated expressed growing annoyance over the noise of aircraft flying over his home, especially at night. As darkness is falling, he tells you that he just received a green laser pointer he bought online, and tonight he's going to use it to teach those pilots a lesson. What will you do, and why?

Online Research Assignments

As assigned by your instructor, prepare to present in class or post online one or more of the following research assignments, including hyperlinks to all online resources relied on:

1. Determine whether the U.S. has enacted any federal law banning or regulating the sale, purchase, possession or use of green laser pointers. If so, identify the offenses provided and penalties for violations.

2. For a nation or union of nations other than the U.S., determine whether there are any legal restrictions in place on selling, buying, possessing, using or aiming green laser pointers at aircraft. If so, describe the offenses specified and penalties for violations.

3. Determine whether the U.S. has adopted any regulations or criminal laws affecting the sale, purchase, possession or use of GPS jammers. If so, describe the actions prohibited and penalties for violations.

4. For a nation or union of nations other than the U.S., determine whether any regulations or criminal laws affect the sale, purchase, possession, or use of GPS jammers. If so, describe the actions prohibited and penalties for violations.

5. Determine whether the U.S. has enacted any federal criminal law relating to the possession or operation of civil unmanned aircraft. If so, describe the actions prohibited and penalties for violations.

6. For a nation or union of nations other than the U.S., determine whether any criminal laws exist relating to the possession or operation of unmanned civil aircraft. If so, describe the actions prohibited and penalties for violations.

7. For a U.S. state, identify any state criminal laws affecting the possession and operation of unmanned aircraft. Describe actions prohibited and penalties for violations. Is this law preempted by any federal law? Explain.

8. Describe recent technological developments in airport pre-boarding screening and evaluate how airline passengers view or are likely to view implementation of each such new technology.

PART V

Labor and Employment Law

16

LABOR AND EMPLOYMENT LAW, GENERALLY

Review Questions

1. As a general rule, an employer can fire an employee at will for what reasons?

2. Under the Civil Rights Act, employers may not discriminate on the basis of what *"protected classes"* in employment and compensation?

3. May employers lawfully refuse to hire a person of homosexual orientation if the person is qualified for the job?

4. May an employer lawfully give preference to a younger person over an equally qualified older person in hiring, compensation, and advancement?

5. A regional airline has advertised openings for aircraft dispatchers. A qualified applicant appears for a job interview in a wheelchair, having permanently lost the use of her legs as a result of a lower back injury suffered in a motorcycle accident. The interviewer, who has never really known anyone with a disability, worries that it would be more difficult for her to get to and from work and to maneuver between the desks in the office. The interviewer also believes the applicant would have difficulty handing flight documents to air crews across the dispatch office counter, which is chest-high to a standing person of average height. Besides, the interviewer feels generally uncomfortable around the person and thinks that the pilots would, too. Can the airline lawfully give hiring preference to another qualified applicant who has no disability? Explain.

6. A Midwestern manufacturer of civil aircraft is hiring janitorial workers to keep the plant clean. Most residents of the area are white and of European descent. The state gave the manufacturer tax breaks valued in millions of dollars to locate in the area, to bring in jobs to replace declining farming jobs. Many applicants for the jobs look and sound foreign to the interviewer and were born in Central and South American countries.

    a. Can the employer lawfully give preference to applicants who were born and raised in the local area over other qualified applicants who came from abroad? Why?

    b. Is the employer allowed to require proof of identity and verify that persons hired are legally qualified to work in the U.S.? Why?

7. Your company is bidding for its first federal government contract. If you are the successful bidder, will this impose additional requirements on your hiring practices? Explain.

8. What is an *"exempt"* employee?

9. You are hired to manage an established FBO. Among the employees under your supervision is a salaried accounts receivable clerk whose duties include maintaining the accounts receivable ledger and routinely billing customers for aircraft rentals, flight instruction, hangar rental, tie-down rental, fuel, and maintenance. Billing is done monthly, and the clerk prefers to work 12–16 hour days for a week to get the bills out, then take several days off to catch up on personal tasks before returning to work to accomplish her other duties. She was one of the company's first employees when it began doing business 15 years ago. The company has always permitted her to work this way. She has never requested or been offered overtime pay. She states that she much prefers the time off instead of money. Is this an acceptable practice? Explain.

10. You are the chief pilot for an air charter company serving primarily an oil industry clientele. Most of your company's flying involves transporting "roughneck" crews of oil workers to and from offshore drilling platforms and other remote and primitive drilling and exploration locations. Weather, duty time, and mechanical considerations sometimes require aircrews to stay at the work site with the workers for overnight or longer. Although you are a male and a seasoned former military aviator with considerable overseas combat experience, the language and behavior of these workers is sometimes too crass for your comfort.

    a. Business is good and the company is accepting applications to hire a dozen additional pilots. Several qualified female aviators apply. You can't imagine exposing women to these rowdy passengers and crude working conditions. You explain the situation and your concerns to each of the female applicants during their job interviews, but they are undeterred. Can you lawfully exclude them? Explain.

    b. The company hires several of the women pilots to fly both helicopters and business jets. A few weeks later, one of them complains to you that when she and a male pilot landed on one of the drilling rigs and deplaned to have lunch, she was subjected to a continuous barrage of whistling and sexually suggestive remarks from a crowd of leering, ogling oil workers. She reports that the other pilot joined in the spirit of the occasion, patting her on the butt while smiling and waving at the workers. She slapped his hand away and told him in no uncertain terms that he did not have permission to touch her but he just laughed and told her to lighten up and enjoy the attention. She was afraid for her personal safety. What will you do? Why?

11. You are the executive vice president of a major flight training company. There is talk of union organizing among the company's flight and simulator instructors. The CEO calls a meeting of company executives to discuss the situation. He expresses a feeling of betrayal that they would do this, "after all I've done for them," and the fervent desire to prevent the unionization of these employees.

   a. One executive recommends the company fire the three instructors they believe to be the leaders of the movement, and then call a meeting with the rest of them and tell them that if they persist in the union organizing effort, they will also be fired and replaced. Is this a good idea? Why? Do you have a better approach to recommend? If so, what?

   b. Several of the instructors express strong opposition to the union organizing effort. Union proponents tell them that if they know what is good for themselves and their families, they'd better shut up and get on board. They and their children are called derogatory names and receive anonymous threatening letters and phone calls, and their personal vehicles are damaged in the company parking lot. Is this lawful? Explain.

   c. Following a bitterly contested organizing effort, the union succeeds in being elected as the collective bargaining representative of the company's instructors. The CEO is now so angry that he says he will never negotiate with union representatives. Is that a real option? Explain.

12. FAA air traffic controllers are getting fed up with their managers, who they say behave in an arrogant and arbitrary manner, treating them like children at best or slaves at worst.

   a. Do the controllers have the right to bargain collectively through their union, NATCA, with the federal government over their working conditions? Why?

   b. If collective bargaining fails to lead to improved working conditions, do the controllers have the right to strike? Explain.

Online Research Assignments

As assigned by your instructor, prepare to present in class or post online one or more of the following research assignments, including hyperlinks to all online resources relied on:

1. Select a U.S. state and determine whether it is a right-to-work state. Analyze the effect of that state's choice on its economy.

2. For a nation or union of nations other than the U.S., identify the law(s) governing labor unions and collective bargaining, particularly as they apply to commercial air carriers and aerospace manufacturers. Compare and contrast those laws with U.S. laws described in this and the following chapters.

3. Identify a particular job with a specific U.S. aviation or aerospace manufacturing company and analyze whether a person employed in that job is entitled to receive overtime pay under the FLSA.

4. For a nation or union of nations other than the U.S., identify the law or laws (if any) regulating employees' hours worked and compensation earned. Compare and contrast these to the U.S. laws on that topic discussed in this chapter.

5. Determine the current U.S. national minimum wage and, for a state of your choice, any current state minimum wage. If the state has a minimum wage lower than the federal standard, which one applies to employers for workers in that state? Explain. If the state has a higher minimum wage than the federal standard, analyze the effect of that higher rate on the state's economy.

6. For a nation or union of nations other than the U.S., identify laws setting minimum wages employers are required to pay employees. Compare and contrast these laws to U.S. law on this topic.

7. Identify and describe a current or recent union-organizing campaign at a U.S. aerospace company, including:

   a. The craft of workers involved;

   b. The plant location involved;

   c. The labor union seeking NLRB certification to represent those workers;

   d. The outcome or status of the organizing effort.

8. Identify a U.S. aerospace manufacturing plant that is operating with no labor union certified to represent any of its employees at that location and no union organizing effort known to be underway. How long has that plant been in operation? Identify factors you believe account for that plant being non-union.

17

AIR CARRIER LABOR LAW

Review Questions

1. What law governs labor-management relations in the airline industry?

2. What was Congress's purpose in enacting that law?

3. What federal administrative agency has the responsibility for overseeing labor-management relations in the airline industry under that law?

4. Does the statutory and regulatory structure described in your answers to questions 1–3 above apply to any non-airline aviation companies? Explain.

5. You and your fellow pilots employed by an airline whose pilots are not represented by a union are dissatisfied with your pay scale, working conditions, and other company policies. Many of you have expressed your opinions on these subjects to the company's management, without result. You believe that there is enough frustration and discontent among the pilots that they would like to be represented by a union. How could a union get the authority to represent the airline's pilots? Describe.

6. You are an aircraft mechanic for an airline whose mechanics are represented by a labor union. You don't like unions, don't want to pay union dues, and would rather negotiate your own deal with management instead of having to be bound by the union's contract. Can you opt out? Explain.

7. You are a union representative for an airline's pilots. The company's check airmen were found by the NMB to be "labor" (rather than "management") and are now union members. You know that all the check airmen were strongly opposed to unionization of the pilots and lobbied the other pilots vigorously to try to convince them to vote against the union when the election was held. You know that they are still opposed to the union and continually "bad-mouth" it. The union is now in the process of negotiating a new contract with the airline, and it occurs to you that you now have the opportunity to get back at these check airmen for their anti-union activities by trading off some of their pay and benefits in contract negotiations. Would that be legal? Explain.

8. You are a pilot for a regional airline. Starting the twin-engine turboprop to get some heat to warm the cabin for a predawn departure on a bitterly cold winter morning on an unlighted ramp, you are startled by a loud noise from the vicinity of the left engine and shut it down. It turns out that the company's ramp agent had left a passenger's dark-colored bag on the dark ramp near the left engine and the bag (which you had not seen) was sucked into the propeller when you started the engine. The passenger's bag and contents were ruined, the propeller was damaged requiring repair, and the flight was required to be cancelled because no backup aircraft was available. The company fires you.

    a. If the company's pilots are represented by a union and working under a contract, do you have some right to appeal that decision? If so, describe the typical appeal procedures provided by such union contracts.

    b. Will the union provide you with representation on that appeal? If so, describe.

c.   If the company's pilots are not represented by a union, meaning no collective bargaining agreement is in place, do you have the right to appeal your firing? Explain.

9.   A particular airline employee is generally disliked by everyone in the company, labor and management alike. One day the employee violates a company rule and is fired. The employee files a grievance with the System Board of Adjustment under the provisions of the union contract with the company. You are one of the union representatives on the System Board. You and the other union member of the board are walking down the hall in the company's offices when one of the company's representatives on the board calls you into his office. The other company member of the board is already there. Closing the door behind you, one of the company board members says: "As long as we are all here, why don't we have a quick System Board meeting and dispense with that grievance so none of us will have to put up with that jerk anymore?" If the grievance is decided at this impromptu meeting, without notice to the employee, is there anything the employee can do about it? Describe.

10. The contract between the pilot's union and an air carrier has reached its amendable date. Company management decides that unless pilot salaries are immediately reduced by 25%, the company will be unable to compete effectively against its major competitor (which has the advantage of using cheaper nonunion labor).

a.   What procedure must the company follow before it can start issuing smaller paychecks to its pilots? Why?

b.   In the first conference between company management and union representatives, the management negotiator states: "There is no alternative to this 25% pay cut. It is not negotiable. We're not even going to talk about alternatives. Take it or leave it." Is this legal? What recourse does the union have if the company takes this position at this stage?

c.   If the carrier reduces pilot paychecks without first going through the entire procedural process that you described in your answer to part a, above, what can the union do about it?

d. The carrier is following the prescribed procedures, but some of the pilots are so angry that the company would even ask them for this concession that they start a "wildcat" strike (without the union's authorization). The carrier needs these pilots to return to work to meet the company's commitments. What can the carrier do about this wildcat strike?

e. The union calls a strike before all of the prescribed procedures have been completed. The company needs the pilots to return to work to meet its commitments. What can the company do about this union-organized strike?

f. Once the entire procedural process has been completed without a resolution of the dispute,

   i. Is the company free to reduce pilot pay?

   ii. Is the union free to strike?

11. An airline's pilots are not represented by a union. The company has previously scheduled pilots to fly 10 fewer hours per month than the maximum permitted by the FARs. In an effort to improve employee productivity, the company wishes to increase each pilot's required monthly flight time to the maximum permitted by the FARs. Can the company immediately and unilaterally impose the requirement for additional flight time or must it follow some procedure before implementing this change? Explain.

12. Compare and contrast the two fundamental approaches to collective bargaining. Which of these is more likely to achieve the best result for both the company and the union in today's economy? Why?

13. Employees of a legacy airline have been represented by labor unions since well before deregulation, and there is a long history of distributive bargaining between the company and its unions. Identify factors in that history that would make a transition to an integrative bargaining approach difficult.

Online Research Assignments

As assigned by your instructor, prepare to present in class or post online one or more of the following research assignments, including hyperlinks to all online resources relied on:

1. For an air carrier covered by the RLA, identify and describe a current or recent union organizing campaign, including:
   a. The craft of workers involved.
   b. The labor union seeking NMB certification to represent those workers.
   c. The outcome or status of that organizing effort.

2. For an air carrier covered by the RLA, identify and describe a current collective bargaining negotiation, including:
   a. The craft of workers involved.
   b. The labor union representing those workers.
   c. Whether the negotiation involves a new (first) collective bargaining agreement or changes to an existing agreement.
   d. The subjects being negotiated (wages, benefits, working conditions, etc.).
   e. How long negotiations been underway?
   f. Whether the parties are taking a distributive bargaining or integrative bargaining approach.
   g. The current stage of this major dispute in the RLA "Kabuki Theater" process.

3. For an air carrier covered by the RLA, identify and describe a current or recent strike, including:
   a. The craft of workers involved.
   b. The union representing those workers.
   c. The issues involved (wages, benefits, working conditions, etc.).
   d. How long negotiations had continued in the RLA "Kabuki Theater" process before the parties were released to self-help.
   e. The outcome or status of the strike.

4. For an air carrier of a nation or union of nations other than the U.S., identify and describe a current or recent strike, including:

   a. The craft of workers involved.

   b. The union representing those workers.

   c. The issues involved (wages, benefits, working conditions, etc.).

   d. How long negotiations had continued before the strike began.

   e. Any laws that forced postponement of the strike.

   f. The outcome or status of the strike.

5. For a recent merger between air carriers:

   a. Identify the air carriers involved.

   b. Identify a labor union representing either the pilots, mechanics, or flight attendants at each carrier before the merger. (If employees in the craft you select were not represented by a union before the merger, indicate that.)

   c. Identify the surviving carrier.

   d. Identify the labor union representing that same craft of employees selected in b. above, following completion of the merger.

   e. Determine how long it took between the merger agreement and completion of consolidation of operations under the operating certificate of the surviving carrier.

   f. Identify factors that delayed or expedited consolidation of operations under the operating certificate of the surviving carrier.

6. Identify a U.S. air carrier that is currently operating with no labor union certified to represent any of its employees and where no union organizing effort is known to be underway. How long has that carrier been in operation? Identify factors you believe account for that carrier being non-union.

7. Identify an air carrier of a nation other than the U.S. that is currently operating with no labor union certified to represent any of its employees and where no union organizing effort is known to be underway. How long has that carrier been in operation? Identify factors you believe account for that carrier being non-union.

PART VI

Evolving Law

18

COMMERCIAL SPACEFLIGHT OPERATIONS

Review Questions

1. What international law recognizes that the United States and other nations have complete and exclusive sovereignty over the airspace above their territory?

2. Identify the internationally recognized vertical boundary of a nation's airspace (the line of demarcation between airspace and space) and describe the rationale behind selection of that specific altitude.

3. Identify the treaty that is the basis for international law in space, and describe the key principles and provisions agreed to in that treaty.

4. What 1996 event is credited with setting into motion events leading to the birth of the commercial space tourism industry?

5. Identify the primary components and subcomponents of the commercial spaceflight industry.

6. Who won the Ansari X-Prize, when, where, and how?

7. Describe the purpose and requirements of the Commercial Space Launch Amendments Act (CSLAA) of 2004.

8. For U.S. commercial spaceport, space launch and spaceflight operations:

   a. What federal agency and office regulates and licenses these activities?

   b. What law created that office?

   c. What were Congress' purposes in creating that office?

   d. What licenses and permits does that office currently issue?

9. What treaty first specifically addressed international law applicable to property and mineral rights on Earth's moon?

10. What principles are set forth in that treaty?

11. Is the U.S. a party to that treaty?

12. Does any international law specifically address property and mineral rights of businesses seeking to exploit the natural resources of asteroids?

Online Research Assignments

As assigned by your instructor, prepare to present in class or post online one or more of the following research assignments, including hyperlinks to all online resources relied on:

1. Identify current FAA pilot and medical certification requirements for civil spacecraft crewmembers, citing the specific FAR applicable.

2. For a nation or union of nations other than the U.S., identify current legal requirements, if any, for civil spacecraft crewmembers, citing the specific regulation that applies.

3. For one of the companies identified in this chapter as conducting or preparing to conduct commercial space tourism flights, identify and describe the current status of that company's:
   a. Licensing
   b. Launch vehicle(s) and technique(s) (vertical or horizontal)
   c. Spacecraft
   d. Actual commercial cargo- and/or passenger-carrying spaceflights conducted
   e. Additional types of commercial cargo- and/or passenger-carrying spacecraft and spaceflight operations in development.

4. Identify a U.S. company that is not mentioned in this chapter but is now conducting or preparing to conduct commercial space tourism flights. Identify and describe the current status of that company's:
   a. Licensing
   b. Launch vehicle(s) and technique(s) (vertical or horizontal)
   c. Spacecraft
   d. Actual commercial cargo- and/or passenger-carrying spaceflights conducted
   e. Additional types of commercial cargo- and/or passenger-carrying spacecraft and spaceflight operations in development.

5. For a non-U.S. company launching or preparing to launch commercial cargo- and/or passenger carrying spaceflights, identify and describe the current status of that company's:
   a. Licensing
   b. Launch vehicle(s) and technique(s) (vertical or horizontal)
   c. Launch sites used
   d. Spacecraft
   e. Actual commercial cargo- and/or passenger-carrying spaceflights conducted
   f. Additional types of commercial cargo- and/or passenger-carrying spacecraft and spaceflight operations in development.

6. Determine whether rockets and spacecraft designed or used for commercial spaceflight operations remain classified as "defense articles" whose export is controlled by the U.S. Munitions List (USML).

7. Identify and describe current:
   a. International activities intended to further address commercial activities on Earth's moon and/or the asteroids.
   b. Commercial activities underway or proposed to exploit the natural resources of Earth's moon and/or the asteroids.

8. Identify and describe current international activities intended to address the problem of space debris.

9. Identify and describe all reported incidents of spacecraft damage and/or destruction attributed to space debris.

10. Identify and describe current international activities intended to either create a new international organization or expand the role of ICAO to address civil spaceflight operations and challenges.

11. For one of the companies identified in this chapter as conducting or preparing to conduct commercial space launch services, identify and describe the current status of that company's:
    a. Licensing
    b. Launch vehicle(s) and technique(s) (vertical or horizontal)
    c. Flight tests and actual commercial space launches conducted
    d. Additional types of commercial space launchers in development by the company.

12. For a company not mentioned in this chapter as conducting or preparing to conduct commercial space launch services, identify and describe the current status of that company's:
    a. Licensing
    b. Launch vehicle(s) and technique(s) (vertical or horizontal)
    c. Flight tests and actual commercial space launches conducted
    d. Additional types of commercial space launchers in development by the company.

19

UNMANNED AIRCRAFT SYSTEMS OPERATIONS

Review Questions

1. Name the Act of Congress that gave birth to 14 CFR Part 107.

2. How many types of UAS users does the FAA define? Name them.

3. What rules apply to each category of UAS user?

4. Name the rules of 14 CFR Part 107 that are waiverable.

5. What is LAANC and how do you use it?

6. What is urban air mobility (UAM) and what are some challenges to be overcome as they are integrated into the National Airspace System (NAS)?

7. What is "counter UAS" and what are some ways it is carried out?

Online Research Assignments

As assigned by your instructor, prepare to present in class or post online the following research assignment, including hyperlinks to all online resources relied on.

1. Name a company that is currently flying packages for compensation and describe their operations, including any special circumstances that allow them to operate safely within the National Airspace System.

2. How does a company perform UAS operations using a Part 135 certificate obtained through the FAA?

3. Summarize the findings of the Lead Participants in the UAS IPP.

4. For your home state or a state you're interested in, identify and summarize either:

   a. All state laws governing UAS operations, or

   b. A specific city's local ordinances, rules and policies governing UAS operations. (If there are none of either, try another state until you find some.)

5. For a nation or city state other than the U.S., identify and summarize that nation or city state's laws and regulations governing UAS operations.